GW01032777

CARIBBEAN VOICES
An Anthology of West Indian p
Volume 1 DREAMS AND VISIONS

CARIBBEAN VOICES

An Anthology of West Indian Poetry

Volume 1 DREAMS AND VISIONS

Selected by JOHN FIGUEROA

 EVANS BROTHERS LIMITED

Published by Evans Brothers Limited
2A Portman Mansions, Chiltern Street, London W1M 1LE

Evans Brothers (Nigeria Publishers) Limited
PMB 5164, Jericho Road, Ibadan

First published 1966
Reprinted 1968, 1970, 1972(2), 1973, 1977
Second edition 1982
Reprinted 1984, 1985, 1987

Set in 11 on 12 pt Imprint by C. Tinling & Co. Ltd. and printed
in Great Britain by William Clowes Ltd., Beccles and London
ISBN 0 237 50751 X

For
Frank Collymore
Henry Swanzy
Arthur Seymour
Edna Manley
in whose footsteps it is not easy to follow,

And for all who in their various ways have made possible
Bim
The BBC's *Caribbean Voices*
Kyk-over-al
Focus

Acknowledgements

Apart from expressing our deep gratitude to the various authors represented, we are also indebted to the following for permission to use the poems in this anthology: Mrs. Jessie Dayes, executrix for the late Roger Mais; Carl Cowl, Esq, literary agent and executor for the late Claude McKay; Miss Ethel Marson, executrix for the late Una Marson; Messrs Jonathan Cape for 'Greenwich Village, winter' and 'A city's death by fire' from *In a Green Night: poems 1948–1960* by Derek Walcott (Cape, London, 1962); the Oxford University Press for 'June bug' from *Tropical Childhood* by Edward Lucie-Smith (OUP, London, 1961); Mrs. Greta Graham and W. Keith Mitchell, Esq, executors for the late Reginald M. Murray; and Vivian Virtue, Esq, for his translation from the French of 'The Conquistadores' by José-Maria de Heredia.

A special word of thanks is due also to Robert Paul Figueroa for invaluable help in proof reading.

Although every effort has been made it has not always proved possible to trace owners of copyright. However, acknowledgement will be made in a later edition if those concerned will contact the publishers without delay.

Foreword

'The eye makes the horizon'; and this collection of poems quickens the eye and enlarges the horizon.

To my great gain, I was brought up on Tennyson and later Browning and Wordsworth, Keats, and later, Shelley. But something was missing. I knew that I lived in a region of bewitching beauty but I found no poets to open magic casements on my fields of bananas and orange trees in the way that Keats transformed, or Wordsworth illumined, the English countryside. Without knowing why, I felt a little poverty-stricken, a poor relation, because there was no West Indian poet with whom I might walk as I did with the poets of England. I belonged to a people without a literature. There was beauty; my island, like Prospero's, was full of sweet sounds; but why were there no voices?

I discovered how much I had missed when, years later, I first read Claude McKay's poetry, defiant, in New York. It was not great poetry, yet with what magic excitement I read 'So much have I forgotten in ten years'. This was the world that I knew, where ground doves filled the noonday with their curious fluting and honey-fever grass sweetened the air. Here at last was a voice singing of the West Indian countryside as home, here at last an assertion of a West Indian way of life.

Claude McKay died in 1948. His 'Spring in New Hampshire' and 'Harlem Shadows' belong to the 1920's. At that time there were one or two West Indian writers— McKay, C. L. R. James, H. G. DeLisser, but there was no West Indian literature. Not until the early 1940's did the West Indian novel emerge. The first West Indian voices belong to the 1930's. In this sense, then, *Dreams and Visions* is a collection of new work, and it discloses poetry of a remarkable range and variety.

The loved and remembered voices are here: Mais,

Campbell, Collymore, Roach and others. But John Figueroa has enriched our understanding of the better-known writers by including poems hitherto rarely seen in anthologies; such as the lovely 'Children Coming from School' by Roger Mais, and George Campbell's 'Drought'.

And John Figueroa has put us more deeply in his debt by bringing together in this collection a large number of poems that might otherwise, to our great loss, have been forgotten, or even lost because (as he points out) of the circumstances in which West Indian poets have been writing for some time. His voyage through BBC scripts over the past fifteen years has already yielded in this first volume rich cargo, with Ingram's

'It is a rose-red morning,
 Who are those going down the hills?'
and Escoffery's
'I awake to the gift of blue sight
 making the world a blue place'
and Barbara Ferland's 'Ave Maria'. Wisely, also, the editor has widened the circle still more to include islands not English-speaking. Wisely, because the tides that separate island from island in our archipelago run deep with blood and war and Guadeloupe is farther from Barbados than is London; but de Chambertrand brings the French seaside villages close, and José-Maria de Heredia rolls back four and a half centuries to show white caravels that 'Dip under the swift uprising of strange stars'.

I am grateful to John Figueroa for giving me the opportunity of indicating how much this anthology already means to me; and far more grateful to him for bringing Caribbean Voices into the homes and schools of the lands that are ours, from Belize in the far west, and the Bahamas in the north, to Trinidad and Guyana, more than a thousand miles away, to the south-east.

PHILIP SHERLOCK, CBE, BA, LLD,
Formerly Vice-Chancellor, University of the West Indies

Contents

Introduction

These poems are presented to students, teachers and to the general public in the hope that they will afford pleasure and satisfaction, and will open new windows to that marvellous world of fiction and the imagination which is poetry. Without dreams and visions no country can live. For a long time it has been felt that further attempts should be made to present the dreams and visions of our own poets in the Caribbean to the students and the public of our area. This is the first volume of an anthology which attempts to do so.

That this anthology has been planned in two volumes is most important to keep in mind. While it is hoped that both volumes will delight a wide audience, Volume 1 is primarily intended for use in the upper reaches of all-age schools, and in the first four forms of secondary schools. Volume 2 is intended for the secondary school generally, for the general public and for University students who are doing survey courses in West Indian civilisation and culture.

It is quite likely that readers will not find some of their favourite poems in Volume 1. They will, I hope, find them in Volume 2. One or two well-known West Indian poets such as Derek Walcott, Philip Sherlock, C. L. Herbert and E. M. Roach are but slightly represented in this first volume: some others do not appear at all, for instance L. Edward Brathwaite and Louise Bennett. This is because their work is more suitable for Volume 2, where it will appear.

Two major difficulties have confronted me in the selection of the poems. First of all, much of the better-

known West Indian poetry tends to be rather too sophistic-
ated, both in outlook and in treatment, for the 'Lower
School'. The second problem has been one connected with
the circumstances in which West Indian poets have been
writing for some time. Until recently there was no West
Indian publishing house. There were few opportunities to
publish verse regularly; and unfortunately the reading
public for poetry in the West Indies has tended to be
found mainly in schools, where little West Indian poetry
has been read.

The problem was to make certain that all the available
material was carefully examined. In the end the only way
to do this was to get permission of the BBC to go through
some fifteen years of their scripts—especially those of the
programme *Caribbean Voices*. This examination has
meant two special trips to London.

The role played by the programme *Caribbean Voices* in
encouraging West Indian writers at a time when it was,
with the remarkable exception of *Bim*, the sole regular
opportunity for publishing West Indian verse, explains the
title of this anthology. *Bim* is, of course, that remarkable
literary journal which has been produced in Barbados with
regularity for some 22 years now. It was first edited by
Jimmy Cozier and the late W. Therold Barnes. In addition
to Frank Collymore, who has been associated with the
magazine for over twenty years, the present editors are
A. N. Forde, L. Edward Brathwaite and Harold Marshall.
I wish to salute *Bim*, and in an especial way Frank Collymore who has been such an encouragement to all writers in
the West Indies. All who are interested in contemporary
Caribbean writing should read *Bim* regularly.

The generosity of the BBC in allowing me to use their
scripts is here most happily acknowledged. In this connection warm thanks are due to Anthony Martin and
Ronald Hopper of the BBC.

In mentioning *Caribbean Voices* one must pay tribute to
the late Una Marson, who started the programme, and to
Henry Swanzy who for many years continued it with such

energy, critical insight and generosity. George Lamming, in his *Pleasures of Exile*, pays tribute to Henry Swanzy's work in connection with the recent flowering of West Indian fiction; we must here especially and gratefully recall the work which he did on *Caribbean Voices*.

It is necessary to point out that no exclusiveness can be reasonably maintained in the field of poetry, and for this reason, and also to broaden the reading of children in schools, I have, in a series of notes, suggested other poems, not written in the West Indies, or by West Indian poets, which are in some way related to those in this book. Teachers and students, and all other readers, are recommended to look these up. In this way they will add to their enjoyment, and realise that man everywhere has his dreams and visions, even though ours are evoked in a special way, and with a special savour, by Caribbean voices.

JOHN FIGUEROA, AB (Holy Cross), MA, TD (Lond.), LHD (Holy Cross),

Introduction to Revised Edition

I am very happy that a revised edition of *Dreams and Visions* is being issued. The fact that the book is being used for a Caribbean examination should in no way lessen the pleasure and insight which it can afford especially to Caribbean Heritage people, whether they live at home or abroad.

I have taken the opportunity to improve the section on the poets whose work has made this book. One hopes that the reader will note the width of their background, born as they are all over the Caribbean and in North America and Europe.

The section on further reading of Caribbean authors (page 110), has been enlarged to take account of the expansion of Caribbean poetry since 1966 when *Caribbean Voices* Volume 1 was first published. There are many other authors and books which could have been mentioned, had space allowed, as a glance at *Caribbean Writers*[1] will prove. Teachers and students alike will find that large reference book interesting and useful, as they will a careful look at *Caribbean Voices* Volume 2 and its extended introduction.

I hope that those who are now using *Caribbean Voices* as an examination text will enjoy *Dreams and Visions*; the special study that they give to it should increase their pleasure and insight, and lead them to read further fiction whether from the Caribbean, Africa, Europe or the Americas:

'A book is a life . . .'   (page 53)

'sing now, bloom now, another sun will bring another rose, another bird to sing . . .'   (page 55)

JOHN FIGUEROA (Selector and Editor),
Third World Studies, The Open University, England
October 1981.

---

[1] *Caribbean Writers*, Three Continents Press Inc., Washington, D.C. 1979. (Eds: Herdeck, Lubin, J. Figueroa, D. Figueroa, Alcantara).

The riders

Over the hill in the mist of the morning,
I see them a-coming, an army a-wheel;
Four abreast, six abreast, the road keeps on spawning
Them, hard-riding men with faces of steel.

Young men and old men, they ride on together,
None paying heed to the one at his side;
Toe to toe; wheel to wheel. Crouched on the leather
Seats, over their handle-bars, onward they ride.

Grim must their faces be; theirs is the ride of life;
Bread's at the end of it, and leisure to follow;
Bread for a mother or sister or wife,
A toy for the kid, or a kiss in the Hollow.

Out of the distance and into the view they come,
Hundreds of men with their feet on the pedals;
The sweat on their faces; hear how their cycles hum,
Riding for bread, not for glory or medals.

BARNABAS J. RAMON-FORTUNÉ

Children coming from school

I can hear the gospel
Of little feet
Go choiring
Down the dusty asphalt street.

Beneath the vast
Cathedral of sky
With the sun for steeple
Evangeling with laughter
Go the shining ones
The little people.

ROGER MAIS

It is a rose-red morning

It is a rose-red morning,
Who are those going down the hills?
Who are those going under the leaves
Under the bamboo awning?

They are the women going to market
With limes and lemons in wicker baskets:
Beautiful tear-shaped limes and lemons
Nestling between the sea-green melons.
I held one cupped within my hand
Full of the fragrance of the land
Pointed and pregnant like a breast
As scented and firm it lay at rest.

2

The women have passed beyond the trees
But the scent is entangled in the breeze.
Beautiful lime-green lemon drops
That fell at three in the morning.

K. E. INGRAM

To Schoelcher[1]

I know you only as a name and an image.
For the little slave a bowed forehead: Schoelcher,
your name is a murmur, a beloved stammering
sung by a people on the hills by the coast.

Pitying and guided by our star, O magician
to the sad cradle where wails the flesh of the races
born of the dark Niger River,
you came, with laden arms, in homage,

homage that the strong, the knights of the spirit,
owe to the touching cry of human weakness;
you came dispensing hope to the proscript;

Divine giver of love, abolisher of hatred,
you died, but you live again, in all your benevolence
as we climb toward the summits of enlightenment.

GILBERT GRATIANT
Translated from the French by C. F. MacIntyre

[1] Schoelcher: *Victor Schoelcher* (1804-93.) French politician, son
of a rich producer of porcelain, he worked for many liberal news-
papers. He was converted by a voyage to the U.S.A. and the Antilles
(1829) to the cause of the slaves, and carried on vigorous campaigns in
the press against slavery. While a senator, he showed great interest in
colonial questions and worked for the abolition of the death penalty.

The song of the banana man

Touris', white man, wipin' his face,
Met me in Golden Grove market place.
He looked at m' ol' clothes brown wid stain,
An' soaked right through wid de Portlan' rain,
He cas' his eye, turn' up his nose,
He says, "You're a beggar man, I suppose?"
He says, "Boy, get some occupation,
Be of some value to your nation."

I said, "By God and dis big right han'
You mus' recognize a banana man.

"Up in de hills, where de streams are cool,
An' mullet an' janga[1] swim in de pool,
I have ten acres of mountain side,
An' a dainty-foot donkey dat I ride,
Four Gros Michel,[2] an' four Lacatan,[2]
Some coconut trees, and some hills of yam,
An' I pasture on dat very same lan'
Five she-goats an' a big black ram,

"Dat, by God an' dis big right han'
Is de property of a banana man.

[1] janga: a crayfish, found in some of the rivers of Jamaica.
[2] 'Gros Michel' (pronounced 'grow mee-shell') and 'Lacatan' are two
varieties of bananas.

"I leave m' yard early-mornin' time
An' set m' foot to de mountain climb,
I ben' m' back to de hot-sun toil,
An' m' cutlass rings on de stony soil,
Ploughin' an' weedin', diggin' an' plantin'
Till Massa Sun drop back o' John Crow mountain,
Den home again in cool evenin' time,
Perhaps whistling dis likkle rhyme,

(*Sung*) "Praise God an' m' big right han'
I will live an' die a banana man.

"Banana day is my special day,
I cut my stems an' I'm on m' way,
Load up de donkey, leave de lan'
Head down de hill to banana stan',
When de truck comes roun' I take a ride
All de way down to de harbour side—
Dat is de night, when you, touris' man,
Would change your place wid a banana man.

"Yes, by God, an' m' big right han'
I will live an' die a banana man.

"De bay is calm, an' de moon is bright
De hills look black for de sky is light,
Down at de dock is an English ship,
Restin' after her ocean trip,
While on de pier is a monstrous hustle,
Tallymen, carriers, all in a bustle,
Wid stems on deir heads in a long black snake
Some singin' de songs dat banana men make,

"Like, (*Sung*) Praise God an' m' big right han'
I will live an' die a banana man.

5

"Den de payment comes, an' we have some fun,
Me, Zekiel, Breda and Duppy Son.
Down at de bar near United Wharf
We knock back a white rum, bus' a laugh,
Fill de empty bag for further toil
Wid saltfish, breadfruit, coconut oil.
Den head back home to m' yard to sleep,
A proper sleep dat is long an' deep.

"Yes, by God, an' m' big right han'
I will live an' die a banana man.

"So when you see dese ol' clothes brown wid stain,
An' soaked right through wid de Portlan' rain,
Don't cas' your eye nor turn your nose,
Don't judge a man by his patchy clothes,
I'm a strong man, a proud man, an' I'm free,
Free as dese mountains, free as dis sea,
I know myself, an' I know my ways,
An' will sing wid pride to de end o' my days

(*Sung*) "Praise God an' m' big right han'
I will live an' die a banana man."

EVAN JONES

6

Adina

They hunt chameleon worlds with cameras.
Their guides avoid the virtue of our valleys.
They have not seen Adina's velvet figure
Swimming uncovered in our river's bubbles.
They have not seen the bamboo's slow manoeuvre,
The light refracting round her shapely ankles:
They have not seen Adina's dancing beauty
Blazing effulgent in the Caribbean.

They stalk with telescopes the larger precincts.
Their view ascends skyscrapers' hazy regions.
They have not seen the silver sun on green leaves,
Adina's basket starred with fruit and flowers,
The bird-sung matinee, the dancing palm-trees,
Beside her rhythmic swinging arms and foot stride,
They have not seen Adina in the breezes
Blazing effulgent in the Caribbean.

HAROLD M. TELEMAQUE

Beggarman

That you should come
Crawling
Like a common worm
Into my yard
Ragged and odorous
Screwing up your face
In unimaginable agony
And with a gesture ultimate in despair
Stretch out your hand
Palm upwards
Begging

Go way, I have nothing.
So much for charity
A barefaced slap
Dazed and puzzled he stood
Waiting
Waiting as if that cracked picture of man
Could storm the barricaded conscience
Waiting with walled patience
Go way, I repeated fiercely. Nothing.
Surprise wiped patience
Hurt, surprise
Anger, hurt
It was done
The unpardonable offence committed
I chased from my doorstep
A beggarman
Hungry

And what of the ultimate insult to manhood
Committed by this scarecrow
Why in this vast and vaunted freedomage
Should he
Wearing the rags of his decayed inheritance
Self-pitying, self-humiliating

Face furrowed with a thousand years
Of trampling on
Why come to stand before me
A mocking testament
Even my dog begs with more dignity

You scarecrow in my yard
Your grotesquerie is a lie
Carved on the conscience of time
That we are brothers
You deny the wasted manhood
Coursing your stiff bones
If you want what I have
Earn it
Lie rob burn kill
Assert your right to life
Win the shuddering admiration
Of a world grown weary with humility
But do not, do not
Stand there
A broken dumb image of a man
Palm upstretched
Accusingly
You'll get no judgment here

So he turned away with his hurt angry look
Ill-masking hate
Went out my garden gate like a sick dog
Empty
And in my pocket burned
Three bright red pennies
And in my bones
A twisted agony
Go way
I hate you
Brother

ERROL HILL

Marketwomen

Down from the hills, they come
With swinging hips and steady stride
To feed the hungry Town
They stirred the steep dark land
To place within the growing seed.
And in the rain and sunshine
Tended the young green plants,
They bred, and dug and reaped.
And now, as Heaven has blessed their toil,
They come, bearing the fruits,
These hand-maids of the Soil,
Who bring full baskets down,
To feed the hungry Town.

DAISY MYRIE

The modern man

I came
And laughed at my father—
He
with his sideburns
Smelling of bear's grease
His coat
like that of the gentleman
whose image
is on tobacco tins
His watch-chain
And boots!
God!
how ridiculous he looked!

I
With my moustache
like Gable's
My sports coat
like Taylor's
My blue suede shoes

Today
My son came
And laughed at me.

BASIL McFARLANE

The shoemaker

I awake to the gift of blue sight
making the world a blue place,
full of flowers.
The lily in my backyard gleams through a haze
of smoke.
In the morning the wind rises,
Blowing in at my doorway many customers
and one old saying:
*"Every fool knows that a man's foot
Is nobler than his shoe"*.

GLORIA ESCOFFERY

Negro lass

Hear the crash of the jungle trees.
Sway to the ground and bend your knees
Out in the clearing here she comes,
Negro Lass with the skin of pearl,
Black as jade, and a jade, this girl,
Blow the conchee, beat the drum,
Beat my heart, beat to your doom,
Beat the drums, beat!
    Boom-boom! boom-boom!

Heart of a savage, eyes of a star,
Lithe as a panther. Africa!
Fierce as a tigress, and as bold,
Warm as the jungle and as old.
Dance, like an Amazon gone mad,
Though a world should burn, dance, and be glad.
Life is wild like a frenzied beast,
Life must dance, ere it joins the feast
Beat my heart, beat to your doom.
Beat the drums, beat!
    Boom-boom! boom-boom!

Negro lass! Negro lass!
There's no mamba[1] in the grass,
Roll your eyes; roll your hips,
Roll till the words beat past your lips.
There is a rhythm in my heart
Roll, roll, never to part—
Roll on, sorrow. Roll on, joy.
Roll, roll, Negro Boy!
For I must sing till I die, die,
Burst through the vaulted azure sky.
Beat the drums, beat! Boom-boom! boom-boom!
Beat fast my heart, beat to your doom.

WILLIAM ARTHUR

[1] mamba: This word (said to be of Zulu origin) designates the most dreaded of African snakes.

My mother

Reg wished me to go with him to the field.
I paused because I did not want to go;
But in her quiet way she made me yield,
Reluctantly, for she was breathing low.
Her hand she slowly lifted from her lap
And, smiling sadly in the old sweet way,
She pointed to the nail where hung my cap.
Her eyes said: I shall last another day.
But scarcely had we reached the distant place,
When over the hills we heard a faint bell ringing.
A boy came running up with frightened face—
We knew the fatal news that he was bringing.
I heard him listlessly, without a moan,
Although the only one I loved was gone.

II

The dawn departs, the morning is begun,
The Trades come whispering from off the seas,
The fields of corn are golden in the sun,
The dark-brown tassels fluttering in the breeze;
The bell is sounding and children pass,
Frog-leaping, skipping, shouting, laughing shrill,
Down the red road, over the pasture-grass,
Up to the schoolhouse crumbling on the hill.
The older folk are at their peaceful toil,
Some pulling up the weeds, some plucking corn,
And others breaking up the sun-baked soil.
Float, faintly-scented breeze, at early morn
Over the earth where mortals sow and reap—
Beneath its breast my mother lies asleep.

Last night I heard your voice, mother,
    The words you sang to me
When I, a little barefoot boy,
    Knelt down against your knee.

And tears gushed from my heart, mother,
    And passed beyond its wall,
But though the fountain reached my throat
    The drops refused to fall.

'Tis ten years since you died, mother,
    Just ten dark years of pain,
And oh, I only wish that I
    Could weep just once again.

CLAUDE MCKAY

Chaotic epic

Lonely fisherman
Casting his net into shallow seas
Sings a song
As beautiful as sons of the wind,
Black fisherman,
Bound to eternities of squalor
Becomes a moving silhouette

A fleck of shadow
A song and a cadence of laughter with the wind.

And seagulls on the wing
Swoop down to kiss foam crested waves
And flecked with salted spume
Vanish with rushing tides of wind
Beyond the arm of land
And jagged wound of tangled trees.
Echoes of sharp and broken cries
Are all they leave to greet
New flowing tides of wind,
New arriving flocks of birds,
Black fishermen
And crude rock fisted arm of land.

JAN CAREW

16

In memoriam

A nun for all her holiness dies
Like other people
—No tears or flowers at Christmas
And only sometimes remembrance blossoming
Amid the rank running weeds of her grave.

I try but cannot write my affection
Nor my gratitude tell
In the swift turned phrase the
Close rhymed syllable you would have loved.

—So this my only rosemary
Once more to kneel
Near your nightblack robes
Listening the while
Your voice dreams stories of princes
For the lonely boy.

ALFRED PRAGNELL

Theresa, return to me

Theresa, return to me.
The year's impatient months
Are growing grey.
The sun's bronze eyes
Are hollow and
Sadden the sea's face.
The horizon's lips
Seem dark and dim
In the evening's light.
Theresa, return to me
Return, return to me.
Remember how we
Searched the Erigand Hills
Last January,
And gathered pods
From fallen sand-box trees,
And waded down
The little crystal streams
In search of sly guabins,[1]
Or last July
When curiously we
Plucked the sweetest
Flowers in the land
And stared at blooming
Pouis. And heard
Soul-stirring melodies
From the semp's throat.
Oh, child whose
Innocent smile
Lit my dark world.

KNOLLY S. LA FORTUNÉ

[1] guabins: Tiny fish found in streams in Trinidad. Little boys fish
for them with pins.

Song for Marian

As fish slithering through unruffled pools
Do not consider the water
So you soaring in song
Our crumbling faiths recover.

Hearing as a boy the incredible fiction
Embroidering your name, I went this evening
Parading my colour for an auditorium's gaze
To autograph your fame and to record
In language my desire no longer dictates
Your image in song.

I cannot truly remember
Where memory and imagination meet
Or sift the associations that cluster
And crowed the song we greet.

It may have been the music of feathered emissaries
        at carolling dawn,
Or the green lamb's threnody in a deepening chill,
It may have been the hum of sea at sundown,
Or the innocence of tears in the cradling years,
Or was it the voice of the river from which we climbed
Reclaiming its limbs in alien lands?

As fish hoisting their freedom
Leap and are gone
So we at the second's command
Met and were one.

Marian, gentlest of creatures from the darkest of
        continents,
What legacy can your art bestow
On those fortunate fools who marvel your excellence?
Or what grave terrors prevent
If love goes out of gear
And the darkest of continents explores its fear?

Often in our green folly
We mocked the celluloid display,
How darkies south of civilization
Clowned their ways to fame,

And sometimes we laughed at tall tales
Burgeoning from the deep, dark south
Or bade our understanding stand neutral
For the bulletins were so unreal.

Now I venturing from scattered islands
To rediscover my roots
Have found an impersonal city
Where your tales are incredibly true,
And I who had never sworn violence
Nor charted courses for the heart's refusal
To white, black, brown at home or afar
Am urged to register with the outlaws.

Where under the sun is our shelter?
What meadow, stream or pool our ally?
What clocks shall register our waiting
Or at midnight ripen our intentions?

Henceforth I decorate my song in sackcloth
For you and islands at anchor in the west
And contemplate our criminals' lone commandment,
Hate thy brother as thyself.

GEORGE LAMMING

February

Trades ardent from the sea
Laugh among the leaves
And are our lovers' hands
Against our faces.

This is the month we love;
The giant immortelles
Splash fire on the hills,
Hold torches in the dells.

The poui trumpets forth
Her golden semi-breves
That break and fall
Against the scattering trades.

The clean-limbed glorisidia
Is in her heliotrope;
The humming bird and bee
Revel in her glory.

In the village dooryard,
In the close cool orchard
The mango sprays her cream
Foam on her mountained green.

Life lolling underground,
Hearing news of spring
Leaps in the floral blood,
Breaks out in beauty dancing.

As broken hopes arise
After a prolonged
Drought season of the spirit
When visions light shamed eyes.

The trade winds blow, and we
In our year long sunny season
As proper farmers tend
Each one his given garden.

The green rains come, and we
Out of our nurtured earth
With hoe and hope and courage
Shall charm high harvest forth.

E. M. ROACH

Fugue

Have seen the summer convex of the wounded sky,
Want to catch it and clutch it and make it sing
Of the wild wind's whisper and the hard-boiled sun
And the blue day kissing my mountain away
Where the hawks dip wing-tipped diving.

Have seen the curved mane of the wind-whipped cane
Want to snap it and squeeze it and make it rain
On the roots of the summer-tree withering
Where my mountain-mouths lie sleeping
And the hawks dip wing-tipped diving.

Have seen the curving prism of the rainbow's shaft
Want to pluck it and plait it and make it bend
To a pattern in the brain of the mountain-top
Where my grief is sighing like a fingered stop
Where the hawks dip wing-tipped diving
And the graves are green at the world's end.

NEVILLE DAWES

Blue agave

Along the barren hillside strewn,
Scotched between stones, rooted in rock;
Thriving in drought and seablast,
Mysterious, aloof, blue-pale
As the first stain of dusk, impenetrable.

The bunched fingers spiked, at first
Resentful, now drooping as fountains drip,
Resignedly; reptilian leaves armoured
Against the unknown foe, thrusting
Jagged shadows along the sunbaked soil.

Avid the pronged claws, the idle
Teeth; and the uncoiling leaves, stark
And impervious as shark's hide, bear
The imprint of tooth and claw upon them,
Formidable insignia of strange ancestry.

Armoured against forgotten fate
They score the low horizon, fronting
The long deliberate curve of the bay;
Holding within their pale blue depths
Their hoarded secret, their savage beauty.

FRANK COLLYMORE

Nature

We have neither Summer nor Winter
Neither Autumn nor Spring.

We have instead the days
When gold sun shines on the lush green canefields—
Magnificently.

The days when the rain beats like bullets on the roofs
And there is no sound but the swish of water in the
    gullies
And trees struggling in the high Jamaica winds.

Also there are the days when the leaves fade from off
    guango[1] trees
And the reaped canefields lie bare and fallow in the
    sun.

But best of all there are the days when the mango
    and the logwood blossom.

When the bushes are full of the sound of bees and
    the scent of honey,
When the tall grass sways and shivers to the slightest
    breath of air,

When the buttercups have paved the earth with
    yellow stars
And beauty comes suddenly and the rains have gone.

H. D. CARBERRY

[1] Guango: This is the usual name in Jamaica; more commonly
known in other parts of the Caribbean as saman: "[Native name.] A
tropical American tree of the bean family *Pithecolobium saman*, the pods
of which are used as cattle fodder." [*New English Dictionary*].

Night comes

Night comes to this land
Stealing over the windowsills
Of the world.

Swiftly comes the night
And now have her bare feet touched
The dim terraced roofs.

All beneath her
The streets lie
Like rivers of light
Curled.

Night smiles
And soft is her breath giving thanks
For these her proofs.

The white credentials of herself she wears
Her saried
Still
Unanswerable stars.

ROGER MAIS

26

Spring

Do you know why the sun shines
And the breeze throws
Small seeds across the sky?

Do you know why the seas heave
And the young sing
Small songs without a sound?

The universe spins, the world reels, and I
See the street shining. Upside down
You are steady—or do you spin too?

GLORIA ESCOFFERY

Litany

I hold the splendid daylight in my hands,
Inwardly grateful for a lovely day.
Thank you life.
Daylight like a fine fan spread from my hands,
Daylight like scarlet poinsettias.
Daylight like yellow cassia flowers
Daylight like clean water
Daylight like green cacti
Daylight like sea sparkling with white horses
Daylight like sunstrained blue sky
Daylight like tropic hills
Daylight like a sacrament in my hands.
Amen.

GEORGE CAMPBELL

A leaf from the tree of darkness

A leaf from the tree of darkness,
That grows in the midnight still
You floated to me from dreamland,
You poised on my window sill.
Out of the darkness you drifted
And circled around my light,
Drawn by the glare and the brightness
Out of the gardens of night.

A handful of beating softness,
Two eyes that sparkle and glow,
Wings that are covered with gold-dust,
You tremble and flutter so.
You will beat your downy pinions,
You will lie all broken and dead,
If you heed the lure and sparkle
Of the bright lights overhead.

I hold you now as a captive,
Brown leaf from the midnight tree.
And still you flutter and struggle
In your efforts to be free.
So taking you to the window,
I cast you into the night,
Where the soft winds are at vespers
With the stars for tapers bright.

CONSTANCE HOLLAR

We who do not know the snow

We who do not know the snow
And the white teeth of the cold,
Who are not friendly with the quick turn of the
    season,
And the chill inability of the summer plaid,
Still know the light bright cotton cushioning the
    breeze;
Not cold but warm in the drowsy pillow,
Lazy under the blanket, steeped in the drug of night;
Untrampled by passing foot blow . . . .

Now the clouds are a flock of sheep
Grazing over the fertile vault, and the fishermen
    sweep
Over the high home of the fishes, down in the tall
    ditches
Of the sea chasing through mossy reef and coral the
    inhabitants
Of the salt kingdom, seeking flesh to silver dinner
    dishes.

The uncertain seine, a bundle of nerves, molests the
    sad sand,
Twitching with its wet colony as dawn catches the
    strands
Of morning in a ribbon of light and the glad embrace
    of her hand
Hugs archipelago of ships and the ripples dimple with
    brine the planks.

DANIEL WILLIAMS

29

Trees

Trees in the white tide of the lambent moon,
Aloof, austere and proudly swaying trees,
Backwards and forwards swaying in the breeze,
Swaying in the surge of the breeze and sighing tune
On tune, soft songs that breathe awhile, then swoon
Upon the azure silences. O seas
Of silver foliage—O myriad leaves,
O utter beauty of this vast festoon!
Trees in the night, mysterious, dim and wise,
With calm majestic loveliness. I think
They catch the secret that embosomed lies
Within the wind, blown from the sky's lone brink,
As, ever straining upwards, they aspire
To paint their leaves with shimmering star-gold fire.

HAROLD WATSON

An old woman

All other trees were clothed in leaves,
But gaunt against the staring moon
The cashew thrust its ragged limbs,
Each impotent,
Since life had fled;
And silent midst the laughing youth
I saw her gnarled and ancient face,
Expressionless and dead.

P. M. SHERLOCK

Terre-de-Hauts-des-Saintes

The clarity of morning smiles on the landscape.
The chameau[1] before us offers her hump;
on the charming bay and in the enchanted air
a flight of pelicans traces a foreboding presage.

The coast is splendid, odorous and wild;
all along the road the dread cactus raises
his sharpened arrows, and the coming summer
will set shavings of silver on the well-behaved
     Atlantic.

At the end of the happy gulf a bright fisher village
lies with green hills of glittering whiteness
and the Angelus tinkles in a strange setting.

And down there, in the south, through the haze,
above the picturesque brown rocks, under blue skies,
one sees the town of Dominique turning blue.

GILBERT DE CHAMBERTRAND
Translated from the French by C. F. MacIntyre

[1] Chameau: French; means, literally, *camel.*

Darlingford

Blazing tropical sunshine
On a hard, white dusty road
That curves round and round
Following the craggy coastline;
Coconut trees fringing the coast,
Thousands and thousands
Of beautiful coconut trees,
Their green and brown arms
Reaching out in all directions—
Reaching up to high heaven
And sparkling in the sunshine.
Sea coast, rocky sea coast,
Rocky palm-fringed coastline;
Brown-black rocks,
White sea-foam spraying the rocks;
Waves, sparkling waves
Dancing merrily with the breeze;
The incessant song
Of the mighty sea,
A white sail—far out
Far, far out at sea;
A tiny sailing boat—
White sails all glittering
Flirting with the bright rays
Of the soon setting sun,
Trying to escape their kisses,
In vain—and the jealous winds
Waft her on, on, out to sea
Till sunset; then weary
Of their battle with the sun
The tired winds
Fold themselves to sleep

And the noble craft
No longer idolized
By her two violent lovers
Drifts slowly into port
In the pale moonlight;
Gone are the violent caresses
Of the sun and restless winds—
She nestles in the cool embrace
Of quiet waves
And tender moonlight
Southern silvery moonlight
Shining from a pale heaven
Upon a hard, white, dusty road
That curves round and round
Following the craggy coastline
Of Jamaica's southern shore.

UNA MARSON

Drought

No love in my heart
No love in my tree
And I can go down to the sea
And weep my tears
No laughter in my eyes
No laughter in my mouth
And all the land is gold and dry
Thirsting in drought.

GEORGE CAMPBELL

Weather in action

Calm weather is for calm souls;
But the light that comes through the whirling trees
When the wind is high
Stirs the blood of the wild creatures,
Who dance to the rhythm
And sing with the singing leaves.

Weather in action
And the heart bounding—
Joyful outcry, mocking the wail of the wind!

Calm weather is for calm souls;
But the soul of the outcast
Gathers wild weather into itself
And rides the rim of the world!

MARY LOCKETT

Mid-year

Mid-year,
And the confetti-petals of the June rose
Tremble upon the slightest benediction
Of each vagrant breeze,
Tremble and fall,
Like pink and white bits of tissue
Upon the flowerbeds beneath.

Christmas,
It was the incendiary poinsettia
That lit a fire round my garden fence—
Easter,
The rarest resurrection lily,
Delicately tinted,
Stuck her timid fingers
Amid the white-washed stones
Of flowerbeds.
Mid-year,
The confetti June Rose,
Trembling on high branches
In the June wind.

Down the street
There is a tree, the Indian Laburnum
That blossoms every year at this same time,
Bold yellow flowers,
Confidently blooming in huge bunches
From the ends of leafless twigs;
No leaves at all, no trace of foliage green,

She is mid-year too,
This naked tree
And my June Rose
Trembling in the dry June wind.

CARL RATTRAY

Hibiscus

I see her walking in her garden in the morning,
    Her feet follow her eyes to where
    hibiscus grows
Her hair falls like the night behind her.

Observant and aware she knows
    the bloom awaits her coming.
Nor does it turn its head away.
    Her fingers clasp the stem and pluck
    the sun:
    She wears her flower like a golden day.

BARBARA FERLAND

The pelican

With what precision does the slow-winged pelican
Swing in pendulum flight above the waves,
Or poise, a pendant from the brilliant blue,
To dip and swing where breaker upon breaker raves
And bellows over rocks and fluted sands.
There, its rapacious bill—an arrow flung
Towards an instinct's goal—secures the prey.
Presently, two grey ungainly wings withdraw
Above the rocking waves into their pendulum. Hung
High, high above the tarnished copper bay
The pelican defines again the pattern of its every day.

J. R. BUNTING

St. Andrew Hills

St. Andrew Hills! The gentle words
Engrave a name within my heart.
I shall forever guard these heights
And of their solace claim a part.

My feet may never walk again
The silver tracks that now we climb,
But I shall leave a presence here
That is not bound by space or time.

And when you pause by Mammee Bridge
And hear the lapping music flow,
Be sure my spirit listens too,
And that, far off, attuned I go.

I shall remember this clear sky,
The moon of an unearthly gold,
The look of every shining crest,
The light of every mountain fold.

This is Jamaica now—an Isle
Where I have found a hallowed place,
Walked in the footsteps of the stars,
And gazed on Beauty face to face.

STELLA MEAD

Time for digging

It is the time for digging now
For digging yams on the hillside
For the sweat to fall from the honest brow . . . .

It is the time for singing now
For reaping the crop of our early sowing
To dig for the yam that is swiftly growing
It is the time for digging now . . . .

Come lift the hoe, and fell the blow
On the brown good earth God gave us
And let the blade bear song along
To the ears of those who hear us . . . .

It is the time for digging now
For the sweat to fall from the honest brow . . . .

ARCHIE LINDO

38

Gold are the fruit of night

Gold are the fruit of night,
Golden for laughter. . . .

Star-apples on laden boughs
Little cosmic apples

Gay in the frown of night
Their wise light dapples

I saw one shaken down
From its branch tonight.

It fell without a sound
Far, far out of sight—

Beyond, beyond the rim
Of night's dark bowl;

(God grant that His net was by
Saving its soul!)

Yet why weep for fallen stars—
Fruit of Infinity—

Who planned the orchard there,
Planned their hereafter. . . .

Gold are the fruit of night,
Golden for laughter.

CONSTANCE HOLLAR

Scarlet

A scarlet sun on a scarlet sea,
Flamingoes beamed to their evening tree,
My thoughts swing from the hunt of the day,
Out from the waterside far away.

Like filled flamingoes evening red,
My thoughts sail high with wings outspread,
And I capture the mood of the scarlet ring
That the scarlet scene is fashioning.

And my thoughts are spent upon scarlet blood,
On waging wars in a veinal flood.
But I dream of a limb on a peaceful tree
Across the path of the scarlet sea.

HAROLD M. TELEMAQUE

Over Guiana, clouds

Over Guiana, clouds.

Little curled feathers on the back of the sky—
White, chicken-downy on the soft sweet blue—
In slow reluctant patterns for the world to see.

Then frisky lambs that gambol and bowl along
Shepherded by the brave Trade Wind.

And glittering in the sun come great grave battleships
Ploughing an even keel across the sky.

In their own time, their bowels full of rain
The angry clouds that rage with lightning
Emitting sullen bulldog growls
And then they spirit themselves away in mist and
    rain.

Over Guiana, clouds.

And they go rushing on across the country
Staining the land with shadow as they pass.
Closer than raiment to the naked skin, that shadow,
Bringing a pause of sun, over and across
Black noiseless rivers running out to sea,
Fields, pieced and plotted, and ankle deep in rice
Or waving their multitudinous hair of cane.

It scales the sides of mountains
Lifting effortlessly to their summits,
And fleets across savannahs in its race,
But there are times that shadow falters
And hesitates upon a lake

To fix that eye of water in a stare,
Or use its burnished shield to search the sun,
Or yet as maids do,
To let the cloud compose her hurried beauty
And then upon its way to Venezuela
Across vast stretches where trees huddle close
And throw Liana arms around their neighbours.

Over Guiana, clouds.

Forest night full of drums
Death-throbbing drums
For shining-breasted invaders of the shores.

Immemorial feuds shake hands
And Indians come,
Death's harvests swinging in their quivers.

A cinema of rapid figures
Thrown by wood-torches on the trees,
Impassive faces with passion forcing through,
Then the hard treks, and the long full canoes
Rustling down the river-night.

A horror of nights for Spaniards
Keen arrows biting the throat above the steel
The Indians flitting like actors in the wings
The swamps, the heavy marching, the malaria.

A trail of burnt villages and tortured men and
        treacheries.
Wave after wave, the white-faced warriors
Then weary of war,
The Indians talk trade.

Indians knew the bird calls in the woods
Before Columbus sailed.
The swallow songs—
Arrows of longing for the northern Summer days—

The clamorous-winging wild ducks and the choughs
The merry kiskadees and the pirate hawks
The cries of little frightened doves,
The brilliant and unmusical macaws.
And they can tell the single hours to sunset
By the birds cheeping, cheeping overhead.

This wildwood and untroubled knowledge still
Cradles the dying tribes
For death has laid his hand upon the race.

They know the wisdom of all herbs and weeds
Which one to eat for sickness, which to shun
And which to crush into an oil that pulls
The cramping pains from out the marrow bones.

They hear the river as it courses down
And they can tell the rising of the tide
From river-water lapping, leaping softly
Slapping against the wooden landing-stage.

The impassivity of silent trees becomes their own
And they will watch the wheeling of white birds
For company.

But still they have their dances and at nights,
When the drums trouble the dark with rhythm
The violin takes a voice and patterns the air
And then the Indians find their tribal memories
Of victories and war and dim old journeys
That brought them from beyond the Behring Strait.

III

Kykoveral.[1]
Strange name for stones, a heap of stones,
But a strong name to take imagination
And tie it to a peak in Time.
Above lost plains, drowned by the later names,
The English names which still come creeping in
On the slow gathering of the years.

And the strong name winds up the centuries
And builds again the fort to hold the sentry
Standing upon his picket in the night
Thinking of Holland and of home,
While the full everlasting winds stretch out,
Straight as a board and stiff without a flutter,
The Dutch pavilion overhead.

Then the winds howled and gathering strength, they
    whistled
And hurled their music through the clump of trees
Which bowed and swung their torn and weeping
    leaves
Till the young sentry shivered at his post—
This country, with its clouds like new-washed
    fleeces
Capering gaily on the blue map of the heavens,
And then so suddenly the heavens would fall
And bowels of rain let loose would swamp the earth.

[1] Kykoveral: "The Colony (i.e. British Guiana) was first partially settled between 1616 and 1621 by the Dutch West India Company, who erected a fort and depot at Fort Kyk-over-al (County of Essequebo)." p. 475, *The South American Handbook*, 1965.

Kyk does not appear (in this form) in the Dutch Dictionaries consulted; but does in the Afrikaans—where it is listed as "view": Kyk-over-al, therefore, suggests among other things, a place having a wide or predominating view of the surrounding countryside. (Dutch *Kijk*: look, aspect; *over-al* = over all).

Kyk-over-al is, of course, the name of the journal published by A. J. Seymour in Georgetown, British Guiana. To this journal, West Indian writers are very much indebted, as are readers of West Indian fiction.

Just three months more and then the ship comes in
To bear him home again to the low dykes
The trim, familiar chequerboard of Holland.

Trade has been good this year, the Indians friendly,
And no alarms with messengers of death
Winging from Spanish arms—a quiet year.
Idly his mind slid off into smooth wonder

Upon the Portuguese inscriptions carved
Right on the fort. Strange, that they had been here
Where hadn't those indomitable sailors touched?
Up to the margins of the world. And they
Had pushed back frontiers, made the world grow
        greater
Revealed new oceans with their long swift keels
Slicing the waves in clean and steady power.
They had been everywhere, now a dimmed glory.
Soon too, those English hounds would scent the traces
And Drake and Raleigh would bring their vessels
        bobbing
Upon the Isakepe, ready to plunder,
They were not traders—pirates and robbers.

But the night takes its curtains up, the sun
Warms the chill world and brings the sentry his
        relief.

Strange name for stones, a heap of stones,
But a strong name to take imagination
And tie it to a towering peak in Time.

IV

[This is a long section which describes the arrival of Sir Walter Raleigh in Guiana]

V

Slaves
Humming to the twilight by the shanty door
"Oh Lord Jesus."

Slaves
Pouring out heart-music till it run no more
"Oh Lord Jesus."

Slaves born in hot wet forestlands
Tend the young cane-shoots and they give
Brute power to the signal of the lash
It curls and hisses through the air
And lifts upon the black, broad backs
Roped weals in hideous sculpture.
"Oh Lord Jesus."

Some slaves are whipped
For looking at the Master's grown-up daughters
Picking their way across the compound,
And other slaves for trying to run away.
"Oh Lord Jesus."

Some few found kindly-hearted owners
And they were used like human beings
But those were rare, Lord Jesus.

Before, it was the shining yellow metal
And now, the dark sweet crystal owned the land
And if the chattel and the cattle died
There always would be more to take their place.
Till, in its deep sleep
Europe's conscience turned
And strenuous voices
Broke chains and set the people free.
"Oh Lord Jesus."

But there were other chains and earth was not yet
        heaven
And other races came to share the work
And halve the pay.

VI

So with a stride down to the modern times and
Random villages downing between the plantations
The sea pounding away to break the dams.

And the railway pencils a line to the Berbice River
Villages broaden shoulders and, sugar booming,
Schools spring up suddenly to dot the coast.

Men get eager for the yellow metal, shooting
Down rapids for diamonds and quick wealth,
        returning
Bloated and drunk to paint the villages red.

Plantations thicken, spread, and they web together,
The angry sea batters the concrete defences
Scooping a grave for them to bury themselves.

Bustle and industry on the coasts but inland
Few echoes shake the forests from their silences
And nothing wakes their strong cathedral calm.

A. J. SEYMOUR

Poetry

Sometimes I tremble like a storm-swept flower,
And seek to hide my tortured soul from thee.
Bowing my head in deep humility
Before the silent thunder of thy power.
Sometimes I flee before thy blazing light,
As from the specter of pursuing death;
Intimidated lest thy mighty breath,
Windways, will sweep me into utter night.
For oh, I fear they will be swallowed up—
The loves which are to me of vital worth,
My passion and my pleasure in the earth—
And lost forever in thy magic cup!
I fear, I fear my truly human heart
Will perish on the altar-stone of art!

CLAUDE MCKAY

The Poet's post

Go Poet, by the wide bright bay
Where your lone voice is the light's preserve,
And where is the hour of the beautiful
Dancing of birds in the sun-wind.
Follow poet, the pure space where is your position,
And where the irregular waves had creation.
Beneath is no response by the uncertain river
Whose weeping passion broods the wooded rain.
Here, the two seasons are unevenly divided;
Freedom is encircled with water.
Search for a land above the sunlight,
Find the sky regions clean and immune—
From swift death-shadow of the sea-gull, washed,
From pile on pile of undigested bones, untouched.

HAROLD M. TELEMAQUE

Poem

Words—words are the poem,
The incalculable flotsam;
That which bore them vanished beneath
The hurrying drift of time.

How shall they speak, how tell
Of the ship and the lost crew?
Each plank a splinter,
Each splinter enough for memory?

Words float upon the surface, a broken
Message. And with mild wonder
Whereon shall the finder ponder?
What voyage shall he now essay?

Along the trade routes glide, glimpsing
New lands, old scenes? Or peer
Below the restless surface, discerning,
Tangled among the seaweed and obscured,

A shape that might have been a man?

FRANK COLLYMORE

Discobolus of Myron[1]

Discobolus, Discobolus
Oh late, too late
Thy tension loosens
And thy disc is hurled
Thy falsely balanced beauty
Is our fate
Thy profile, perfect
For this self-slain world
Discobolus, Discobolus
Thy first throw make
Hurl self from self free
And at last awake.

M. G. SMITH

[1] Discobolus of Myron: Refers to the famous statue of the discus
thrower by the equally famous Greek sculptor, Myron.

On hearing Dvorak's 'New World' Symphony

The chestnut trunks are dark
Their massive manes are green
And lightly float on dark
Breathing of music wind.

The white swans sail the pond
Before the music wind,
And arch white necks among
The waving chestnut trees.

The music wind billows,
The dark trunks toss green manes:
The swans have felt darkness
Weave slowly through the waves.

I am kneeling in
A night-fall church beyond
The rings of candle light
Which shake in music wind.

One by one acolytes
Are candles leaving dark
The altar whose candles
One by one flicker out.

The night-fall church is night
Except for sanctuary lamp;
I taste the lamp and know
The song of music wind.

Outside, the church of night
Glows with sanctuary lamps.
As music wind falls off
The quiet pond is bright,

No swans, no ducks, no waves
Of green rippling water;
Only quiet stars
Like clouds lighted by dawn,

Like flowers lighted by Spring;
Only bright stars weaved in
The still pond; the song
Of music makes a silence.

JOHN FIGUEROA

Greenwich Village, winter

A book is a life, and this
White paper death,
I roll it on the drum and write,
Rum-courage on my breath.
The truth is no less hard
Than it was years ago,
Than what Catullus, Villon heard,
Each word,
Black footprints in the frightening snow.

DEREK WALCOTT

How shall I sit in dreamy indolence?

How shall I sit in dreamy indolence,
When circles sure the seasons' sad completion,
Nor pluck one fruit from out the gold repletion
Of Autumn's ripe abundance? To the sense,
A thousand flowers in wayward wild profusion
Burden the trembling air with perfumed breath;
Yet here I linger till the blast of death
Shall spoil the prospect with its dissolution.

Waneth the day—the west is slowly dying
In solemn twilight silence. Ere the night
Consumeth all, I know I am commanded
To garner, yet with unavailing sighing
I squander th' irrevocable light—
And tarry sad of heart—and empty handed.

HAROLD WATSON

the word once spoken

the word once spoken falls upon
the ground and instantly is gone

and like a star that burns, man comes,
clean as a word, or like a flame,

blazing, then instantly is gone
back into silence as he came—

only the breadth of a breath divides
the calm of the sea from the raging tides.

bloom, rose, within your blazing hour!
with darts of fragrance wound the spellbound air!

sing, furious bird, your furious song!
assault the ear of life with your sweet power!

sing now, bloom now, another sun will bring
another rose, another bird to sing. . . .

BARNABAS J. RAMON-FORTUNÉ

A mountain carved of bronze

How curious is language and the web we weave in it
And the sense of colour in it—
What does colour mean to man?
It speaks to him in many languages
Emphasizing danger or seeking friendship . . .

Red of fire that burns or fire that warms
Blue of sea that drowns or bears us on its breast
Black of the storm in a sky still brooding
Or black of the night that brings us sleep
White of dusty earth on a mountain road
Or white of the light that warms and sees.

Black for the colour of mourning
White for the colour of death
Yellow the colour of flowers in spring
Grey the colour of the burnt out hearth
Green the colour of leaves and grass
Symbol of softness and of fertile earth.
Red the colour of blood or passion
Red ambivalent speaks of love or hate
Gold the splendour beloved of fashion
Shadows economy of a nation's fate . . .

Oh the riot of colour in the world of earth
Blackman, redman, brownman, yellow man
Man of colour, man of white . . .
Parrot and peacock, bird and beast . . .
All speak to all in the language of colour
Colours of danger, colours of peace
Colours of friendship or hate or spite . . .

Colour of sun, colour of sea,
Colour of mountain, colour of stream,
Shivering green of humming bird
Thin black wing of hawk
Red of the flaming poincianna[1] tree
Dull mossy brown of alligator's back
Floating by in the silty river
River of fish with silver bellies
And thin black fin of white toothed shark
With palid under-flesh the colour of lizards' legs . . .

World of colour, world of life . . .

And I saw once a mountain carved of bronze
Stand out against a sky of green, bright green . . .
Almost yellow
But shot with red
Like a Chinese silk . . .

And it came to me that that moment was electric
And never again would I see the hills that bronze
The sky that green and red
The sea that blue, and all . . . gleaming like a parrot's
      breast . . .

World of colour, world of life
World of movement, world of life . . .
Parrot and peacock, bird and beast
All speak to all in language of colour
Colours of danger, colours of peace
Colours of friendship, colours of strife . . . .

H. D. CARBERRY

[1] Poincianna: A flowering tree more commonly known in many
parts of the Caribbean as the flamboyant, a word which well describes
its striking colourfulness.
   "Poincianna" is said to derive from a French West Indian Governor
M. Poinci. (The plant is of the family *leguminosi*, suborder *cesalpinaceae*.)

In our land

In our land,
Poppies do not spring
From atoms of young blood,
So gaudily where men have died:
In our land,
Stiletto cane blades
Sink into our hearts,
And drink our blood.

In our land,
Sin is not deep.
And bends before the truth,
Asking repentantly for pardon:
In our land,
The ugly stain
That blotted Eden garden
Is skin deep only.

In our land,
Storms do not strike
For territory's fences,
Elbow room, nor breathing spaces:
In our land,
The hurricane
Of clashes break our ranks
For tint of eye.

In our land,
We do not breed
That taloned king, the eagle,
Nor make emblazonry of lions:
In our land,
The black birds
And the chickens[1] of our mountains
Speak our dreams.

HAROLD M. TELEMAQUE

To the unborn leader

You who may come a hundred years
After our troubled bones are dust,
Farseeing statesman, born to lead,
And worthiest of people's trust,

Turn these few pages in that hour
When by dark doubts you are assailed
Of what it boots to shape their power—
Read what we won and where we failed;

And barb the word with wisdom fit,
And build, O build, where we but dream
Expose, undo, repair, extend,
As you, O master, best may deem.
But whatsoe'er of ours you keep,
Whatever fades or disappears,
Above all else we send you this—
The flaming faith of these first years.

H. A. VAUGHAN

[1] chickens: chicken hawks

59

Seeds of the pomegranate

There is no forgetting the islands, I said.

Another had seen the fishermen
Diving for sea-eggs, far-out, between
The reefs; and watched their women
Sitting cross-legged on shore, fasten
The leaves of sea-grape into cones,
Filled with the orange flesh.

There is no forgetting the islands, I said.
Where the sun has left no shadows.

The arum grows wild—a third remembered—
Up on the mountains: And night-blue
Emperors steal its pollen.
I could have crushed their azure bodies
Against my face and sold their wings
To swarthy merchant-smiths.

There is no forgetting the islands, I said,
Where the sun has left no shadows.
They will fill your eyes with richness

Like sun-flowers fixed in the dark
Of waning moons, they said, we have watched
The evening climb from Teneriffe.
And in the hills behind

The villagers put by their potter's wheels
And washed the red clay from their hands.
There is no forgetting the islands, I said,
Where the sun has left no shadows.
They will fill your eyes with richness
Till they have made you blind.

One said—I have pulled the cactus
When it flowered at full moon;
And in the dark it shone like moonlight.
I played my music with the cactus'
Needles, till the lizards froze,
Making an emerald stillness.

There is no forgetting the islands, I said,
Where the sun has left no shadows.
They will fill your eyes with richness,
Till they have made you blind;
And on your lips will crush bright poisons.

The cocoa-pods—another spoke—
Are coloured like their leaves; the water
Purple and red reflection.
And I have curved my hands around
The coconuts a Negress brought
To drink from the fruit's green bowl.

There is no forgetting the islands, I said,
Where the sun has left no shadows.
They will fill your eyes with richness
Till they have made you blind;
And on your lips will crush bright poisons
That steal the senses, leaving sound.

GEOFFREY DRAYTON

Triptych

I see these ancestors of ours:
The merchants, the adventurers, the youngest sons
    of squires,
Leaving the city and the shires and the seaports,
Eager to establish a temporary home and make a
    fortune
In the new lands beyond the West, pawning perhaps
The old familiar acres or the assured competence;
Sturdy, realist, eager to wring wealth from these
    Barbadoes
And to build, trade, colonize, pay homage to their
    King,
And worship according to the doctrines of the
    Church of England.

I see these ancestors of ours
Torn from the hills and dales of their motherland,
Weeping, hoping in the mercy of time to return
To farm and holding, shuttle and loom, to return
In snow or rain or shine to humble homes, their own;
Cursing the day they were cheated by rebel standards,
Or betrayed for their country's honour; fearing
The unknown land, the fever and the hurricane,
The swamp and jungle—all the travellers' tales.

I see them, these ancestors of ours;
Children of the tribe, ignorant of their doom,
    innocent
As cattle, bartered for, captured, beaten, penned,
Cattle of the slave-ship, less than cattle;
Sold in the market-place, yoked to servitude;
Cattle, bruised and broken, but strong enough to
    plough and breed,
And promised white man's heaven where they sing,
Fill lamps with oil nor wait the Bridegroom's coming;
Raise chorused voices in the hymn of praise.

FRANK COLLYMORE

'Revelation'

Turn sideways now and let them see
What loveliness escapes the schools,
Then turn again, and smile and be
The perfect answer to those fools
Who always prate of Greece and Rome,
'The face that launched a thousand ships',
And such like things, but keep tight lips
For burnished beauty nearer home.
Turn in the sun, my love, my love!
What palm-like grace! What poise! I swear
I prize thy dusky limbs above
My life. What laughing eyes!
    What gleaming hair!

H. A. VAUGHAN

My country grows

My country grows
Struggling towards the sun
Conscious of vast forces
Dimly understood
And unappreciated
Compelling from within and from
    without
To an unknown
Unmapped destiny.

My country grows
Groping blindly
Intuitively
Sometimes unreasonably
Filled with a new awareness
A naïve egoism
A new self-consciousness
That will ultimately
Help it to understand
Others around it.
But it is still young
Be patient
And help my country grow.

H. D. CARBERRY

June bug

Bug like a coffee-bean
Thrown on this tabletop
Beside my paper and pen,
You startle me with your rap.

You, on this hot June night
Which opens window and door,
Come like an intimate
From June of a former year.

Then I, a boy with a book
In a room where a bare bulb glared,
Slept—and struggled awake;
Round me the June bugs whirred.

And, by the inkwell, one
Trundled, a frill of wing
Glinting like cellophane:
On the very lip he clung. . . .

You're off? No reason to feel
That *you*, sir, stand on the brink
Of some disastrous fall
Into a pool of ink.

EDWARD LUCIE-SMITH

65

History makers

Women stone breakers
Hammers and rocks
Tired child makers
Haphazard frocks
Strong thigh
Rigid head
Bent nigh
Hard white piles
Of stone
Under hot sky
In the gully bed
No smiles
No sigh
No moan.

Women child bearers
Pregnant frocks
Wilful toil sharers
Destiny shapers
History makers
Hammers and rocks.

GEORGE CAMPBELL

Constitution Day poem

Give us Thy wisdom
More than ever before
Now that our country
Has passed through the door
To wider freedom.

Hold a people's hand
And give us Thy heart
So that everyman
Lives in the land
And holds dear the part
He must play
To fulfil this day.

Give us Thy glory
In the days ahead;
O let our country
Be proud of its story
When we are dead.

GEORGE CAMPBELL

Consecration of the serpents

Over the blue-green waters, stretching to infinity
The canoes pass like black wings
And, on the east of the cliffs, the waves turn silver
Under the light oar of the sturdy paddlers.

The old chiefs tattooed and white-haired,
Torpid with sun, under the rude tropic,
Covered with eagle feathers and stained with red ochre,
Row slowly towards the shade of the branches.

DANIEL THALY
Translated from the French by C. F. MacIntyre

The Palisadoes Peninsula

The moon lifts o'er the mountain, and lights a
        sand-strip line
Where surf swims silver shimmering and sharing
        breakers drone;
Forlorn on spray-wet beaches the night wind
        moaning creeps;
A shadow, black on whiteness, with loitering motion
        creeps;
It speeds . . . then stops. A lance shoots out and
        stabs;
An Arawak, night-hunting, naked and spearing crabs.

A brigantine rides dipping beneath a tropic moon
With Lethmian plunder laden, sentilla and doubloon,
'Tis Morgan makes Port Royal, and bottles chink
    and clash
And sailormen are cheering to see the shore-lights
    flash;
Clarinda flutters to the pier, a glitter of jingling
    rings,
Agog to greet a rover lad who lot of Moidores brings

The selfsame moon is lamping that curving arm
    tonight,
Fanned by Caribbean breezes and carved for heart's
    delight;
The long wave strikes and shivers, salt winds are
    sighing still,
But now strange sounds are mingling, an airport's
    hiss and thrill,
Along a sea-flanked roadway the gleaming autos flow
Where Indian chevied scuttling crab a mort of years
    ago.

REGINALD M. MURRAY

The Conquistadores

Like noble falcons from their native height
Winging, wearying of their wretchedness,
From Palos de Mogeur they forward press,
Adventurers in search of honour and fight.
They go to seize the fabulous metal bright
Cipango hoards in far-off mines, through stress
Of winds that bend their masts, down loneliness
Of seas unknown fronting the New World's might.

Each set of sun, dreaming an epic rise,
The mirrored burning of the tropic skies
With its mirage of glory charms their rest;
Where the white caravels with leaning spars
Towards the trackless limits of the West
Dip under the swift uprising of strange stars.

JOSÉ-MARIA DE HEREDIA
Translated from the French by Vivian Virtue

Thoughts of Port Royal

Here glory is buried under the fallen stone.
In the dim twilight of the ocean bed
Only the sea crabs crawl the darkened streets,
And in the silent halls
The many-branched candles burn around the
    sleeping,
Forever quenchless, shedding their fitful light.

The bright day falling on the broken houses
Discovers only
The ginger lily's unexpected beauty
Blossoming in the festering desolation—
Perfection of young flesh grown tall and straight,
Sucked upwards by the sun, and full of laughter,
And moulded to the sea's will.

Discovers only these,
And old walls stained by a thousand afternoons,
Remembering their glory.

G. A. HAMILTON

And the pouis sing

In far days in happy shires
In the perfumes that all day creep
From virgin moulds, in the fires
Of a sullen but tolerant sun, deep,
Our roots drilled deep and found
In caverns underground
Sweet water
Rich as the laughter
That slept in Carib eyes before fierce slaughter

Through the soft air falling,
Swifter than the sleek hawk dives
On the dove, on silent wing
Pilfered their cacique[1] lives
At our feet in our shade
Where once they had played
In childhood
Children of the sun
Who prayed to the sun to avenge their blood.

Hostile grew the sun and pitiless
Spear sword arrow of light grew fiery
And in the blindness of their bitterness
Bored bird and beast and tree;
Under the whip of savage winds
And intricate with wounds
Necrotic flesh
Fell fold by fold from flanks
That never before had known the driver's lash.

---

[1] Cacique: *New English Dictionary:* "1555. [Spanish or French cacique = Haytian word for 'lord, chief.'] A native chief or prince of the aborigines in the West Indies, etc."

Old, we are old before our prime
    (Springs of laughter ran dry
And hearts atrophied) and in our time
Have heard lips lift their cry
    To the stone-deaf skies, have seen
      How the hawk has been
      Stripped of pride
    In necessary propitiation;
In vale on hill where slave and cacique died

Have seen from the blood arise
    The cactus, live columbarium
Of the winged tears of indignant eyes,
And from its flowers come
    Dim odours, sweetening the air
      Through the desolate years
      And bringing
    To brittle, barren hearts
Auguries of new days, new faith, bright singing.

CECIL HERBERT

For Christopher Columbus

Music came thundering through the North-East
    Trades
Fuller than orchestras, and bent the masts
All through the nights and made them sorrow-laden

For green-graced islands that the ships had passed.
Each day broke on an ocean like a wheel
Bound to a hub of ships though driving fast.

Deep to the westward under a sky now steel
Blue-gray and fatal, and now sapphire blue
Buttressed with golden evenings men could feel

All of their fears come mellow with the hue.
Behind them lay the far and wistful heights
Of Farro and the Fortunate Islands and they knew

Back of these Spain, and widowed women, and lights
From lovely Palos glittering on the sea.
This ocean's only jewel on the sight

Were foreign stars that happened suddenly
Upon the dark, burnt fiercely through the hours
Then shrank to pale ghosts with dawn's light, eerie

Upon the lightening day, small silverflowers.
Then desolation came upon the crews
The emptiness men feel of crumbled towers,

Spent arrows falling, and the slackening will to do
Of men who wander to the world's edge and fall
In a doom of ocean with winds blowing true

And deep to westward in their office. Sails could
Never hope for Spain once more, they said,
Against these winds—then, marvellous as a tale,

Small birds came singing at morning and they fled
When night approached.
                    Men in the ships took heart
Watching each feathered snatch of song and paid

Eagerest heed. But morning's eyelids parted
On miles of ocean meadow, golden weed
Spotted with berries and showing as if by art
Bright green leaves in the water. Then indeed
The crews made clamour against the Italian's will
Of holding course to India.

II

At night Columbus paced the poop alone.
Hard to hold men to a vision.
                    The faith fails
Sometimes even in the dreamer.
                    Signs, signs.
Today a little branch full of dog roses
Drifted along the ocean's breathing bosom
Imagine roses in ocean
Roses at the edge of the world.

The sea was calm like the river of Seville
A day ago and breeze as soft as April
Made fragrant wing to our weary caravels.

Vision, yes, vision.

I, an Italian
Holding three Spanish crews to an unknown land
After how many desert years,
A young man, poor, dreaming on Ptolemy
With his globe, and the maps of Marinus of Tyre,

And the opinion of Alfraganus the Arabian
That the world is not as large as people think

And living in the pages of Marco Polo
The Venetian fêted once by the Great Khan.

Sometimes dreams harden and blaze into a vision
That leads the man to hostile courts and wars.

Fighting against the Moors—but the vision blazing
In the warrior's head.

                    Answering bald-headed friars

Within the Salamanca Council Room.
What St. Augustine and the sages said
How Adam's sons never had crossed the ocean
And peopled the antipodes—answering friars
With the vision burning.

Man must endure the crumbling powers, the crack
Of another's will but hold his vision fast,
Whip muscle and nerve to keep appointed pace
Drive wheel for westward to the couching sun.

Man must adventure to the Sun's declension
Translate his vision into a tower of fact
Despite the loosening limbs, the unstable powers
Failing about him.

Vision moulds clay into a hero despite the man.
Cuts him to the brains and drives him hungry
To bring an inviolate star down to the earth.
Vision may break a man to make a city,

Vision's an edge to civilisation, carving
Beauty from wilderness and charting seas.
Visionless, man falls back into the animal
With nature striding in her ancient places.

And look, look—look, a light—Quick, Pedro, come.

III

And so they came upon San Salvador.
When the dawn broke, the island floated ahead
Thick with the wind-swayed trees upon the shore.

Men shouted and cried for joy to see instead
Of waving waste of ocean, that tangled green,
The shrub and tree all dark with the bright red

Of foreign flowers on the leaves' glossy sheen.
The ships cast anchor with a triple crash
That startled seabirds, whirred them winging, lean

Neck stretched, to bank upon the trees. The splash
Died quickly into winking patches of foam
Widening out upon the swelling wash.

Men crowded boats. The Indians watched them
    come,
Riding upon the breaking waves to shore,
Until they feared and ran to find their homes

Deep in the woods. His mail Columbus wore
The glittering cloaked in scarlet, and he sprang
Out on the sea-stained sand and kneeling, poured
His heart to God. On that beach dawn there hangs
A heavy caul of reverence, for kneeling there
The others felt vast choirs of angels sang

Within their hearts to hallow them many a year.
Rising up sworded, Columbus spoke again
And claimed San Salvador for the royal pair
Fernando and Queen Isabel of Spain.

IV

He dreamed not that the ocean would bear ships
Heavy with slaves in the holds, to spill their seed
And fertilise new islands under whips
Of many nail-knotted thongs—dreamt not indeed
Massive steel eagles would keep an anxious watch
For strange and glittering fish where now was weed.

He knew not that a world beneath his touch
Springing to life would flower in cities and towns
Over two continents, nor guessed that such

A ferment of civilisation was set down
Would overshadow Europe whence he came.
He could not dream how on the nations' tongue

Discovery would marry with his name.
That to these simple Indians his ships brought doom
For cargo; that the world was not the same.

Because his vision had driven him from home
And that as architect of a new age
The solid world would build upon his poem.

And so the day beginning.

              In the vast Atlantic
The sun's eye blazes over the edge of ocean
And watches the islands in a great bow curving
From Florida down to the South American coast.

Behind these towers in a hollow of ocean
Quiet from the Trade Winds lies the Caribbean
With the long shadows on her breathing bosom
Thrown from the islands in the morning sun.

And as the wind comes up, millions of pale trees
Weave leaves in rhythm as the shaft of sunlight
Numbers the islands till it reaches Cuba
Leaps the last neck of water in its course.

A. J. SEYMOUR

The coral polyp

Let us thank now each polypite
Who laboured with all his tiny might
Through countless aeons till he made us
This little island home, Barbados.

The spider

I'm told that the spider
Has coiled up inside her
Enough silky material
To spin an aerial
One-way track
to the moon and back;
Whilst I
Cannot even catch a fly.

Turkeys

Christmas tidings of good cheer
To turkeys seldom sound sincere.

The butterfly

I always think the butterfly
Looks best against a clear blue sky;
I do not think he looks so good
Pinned down within a box of wood.

The mongoose

The mongoose, to tell the truth, is a troublesome
    sort of creature;
His antipathy to feathered stock is not his only
    distressing feature:
For nobody seems to know with any degree of
    certainty which to choose
Of his plural forms—mongooses, mongeese,
    mongoose or mongooze.

Flying fish

The winged part of the flying fish
Is not required in the dish.

The moth

The moth
Eath cloth.

FRANK COLLYMORE

To the Antilles

If Toulouse charms me, O my lovely Antilles,
it is because like you she has Spanish light,
because the soft beauty of her warm-blooded girls
is the sister of the happy indolence of the Creoles.

How often when crossing the doorsill of their shops
where in winter the oranges of Majorca turn yellow,
a melancholy tune from a guitar
has made me see again the barge being towed into port,

How often in the hot bull-rings
my dream has come back in your clear distances
when one threw flowers to the matador,

and the south wind from Cataluña,
after having touched the roses of Gascony,
recalled to me the fragrance of your golden savannas.

DANIEL THALY
   Translated from the French by C. F. MacIntyre

The tropics in New York

Bananas ripe and green, and ginger-root,
   Cocoa in pods and alligator pears,
And tangerines and mangoes and grape fruit,
   Fit for the highest prize at parish fairs,

Set in the window, bringing memories
    Of fruit-trees laden by low-singing rills,
And dewy dawns, and mystical blue skies
    In benediction over nun-like hills.

My eyes grew dim, and I could no more gaze;
    A wave of longing through my body swept,
And, hungry for the old, familiar ways,
    I turned aside and bowed my head and wept.

CLAUDE MCKAY

Jasmine

Your scent is in the room.
Swiftly it overwhelms and conquers me!
Jasmine, night jasmine, perfect of perfume,
Heavy with dew before the dawn of day!
Your face was in the mirror. I could see
You smile and vanish suddenly away,
Leaving behind the vestige of a tear.
Sad suffering face, from parting grown so dear!
Night jasmine cannot bloom in this cold place;
Without the street is wet and weird with snow;
The cold nude trees are tossing to and fro;
Too stormy is the night for your fond face;
For your low voice too loud the wind's mad roar.
But oh, your scent is here—jasmines that grow
Luxuriant, clustered round your cottage door!

CLAUDE MCKAY

On Broadway

About me young and careless feet
Linger along the garish street;
Above, a hundred shouting signs
Shed down their bright fantastic glow
Upon the merry crowd and lines
Of moving carriages below.
Oh, wonderful is Broadway—only
My heart, my heart is lonely.
Desire naked, linked with Passion
Goes strutting by in brazen fashion;
From playhouse, cabaret and inn
The rainbow lights of Broadway blaze
All gay without, all glad within;
As in a dream I stand and gaze
At Broadway, shining Broadway—only
My heart, my heart, is lonely.

CLAUDE MCKAY

At home the green remains . . .

In England now I hear the window shake
And see beyond its astigmatic pane
Against black limbs Autumn's yellow stain
Splashed about tree-tops and wet beneath the rake.

New England's hills are flattened as crimson-lake
And purple columns, all that now remain
Of trees, stand forward as hillocks do in rain,
And up the hillside ruined temples make.

At home the green remains: the palm throws back
Its head and breathes above the still blue sea,
The separate hills are lost in common blue
Only the splendid poinsettias, true
And crimson like the northern ivy, tack,
But late, the yearly notice to a tree.

JOHN FIGUEROA

Alone

Walk in the Tuileries,
The rain has ceased,
Sunshine released
Pours over rims of rain cloud,
And autumn winds
Are winnowing dead leaves,
From chestnut trees.
Dead leaves
On the footpaths
Like moths caught in the wind's flame,
Whirl crazily.
Walk in the Tuileries,
Alone,
For you are not beside me
To walk across
Sloping shadows of chestnut trees,
To hear the death rattle of leaves
On footpaths,
To watch the whirl of chestnut leaves
Caught like moths in the wind's flame.

JAN CAREW

The lament of the banana man

Gal, I'm tellin' you, I'm tired fo' true,
Tired of Englan', tired o' you.
But I can' go back to Jamaica now. . . .

I'm here in Englan', I'm drawin' pay,
I go to de underground every day—
Eight hours is all, half-hour fo' lunch,
M' uniform's free, an' m' ticket punch—
Punchin' tickets not hard to do,
When I'm tired o' punchin', I let dem through.

I get a paid holiday once a year.
Ol' age an' sickness can' touch me here.

I have a room o' m' own, an' a iron bed,
Dunlopillo under m' head,
A Morphy-Richards to warm de air,
A formica table, an easy chair.
I have summer clothes, an' winter clothes,
An' paper kerchiefs to blow m' nose.

My yoke is easy, my burden is light,
I know a place I can go to, any night.
Dis place Englan'! I'm not complainin',
If it col', it col', if it rainin', it rainin'.
I don' min' if it's mostly night,
Dere's always inside, or de sodium light.

I don' min' white people starin' at me
Dey don' want me here? Don't is deir country?
You won' catch me bawlin' any homesick tears
If I don' see Jamaica for a t'ousand years!

. . . Gal, I'm tellin' you, I'm tired fo' true,
Tired of Englan', tired o' you,
I can' go back to Jamaica now—
But I'd want to die there, anyhow.

EVAN JONES

Spring in New Hampshire

Too green the springing April grass,
    Too blue the silver-speckled sky,
For me to linger here, alas,
    While happy winds go laughing by,
Wasting the golden hours indoors,
Washing windows and scrubbing floors.

Too wonderful the April night,
    Too faintly sweet the first May flowers,
The stars too gloriously bright,
    For me to spend the evening hours,
When fields are fresh and streams are leaping,
Wearied, exhausted, dully sleeping.

CLAUDE MCKAY

Like a strong tree

Like a strong tree that in the virgin earth
Sends far its roots through rock and loam and clay,
And proudly thrives in rain or time of dearth,
When dry waves scare the rain-come sprites away;
Like a strong tree that reaches down deep, deep,
For sunken water, fluid underground,
Where the great-ringed unsightly blind worms creep,
And queer things of the nether world abound:
So would I live in rich imperial growth,
Touching the surface and the depth of things,
Instinctively responsive unto both,
Tasting the sweets of being, fearing no stings,
Sensing the subtle spell of changing forms,
Like a strong tree against a thousand storms.

CLAUDE McKAY

Music a kind of sleep

Music a kind of sleep
imposes on this weary flesh
wind beyond silence
speech of the God who ordered
trees flowering of dark earth
light, essence of darkness
birth

Lucifer massed
in arrogant disorder all about
pale quiet strength of stellar presences
hears in a wonderful dread
music a calm
persistent tread
above the wild torment of nameless waters.

BASIL MCFARLANE

Prayer at morning

Soft rolling cloud who see me here,
A little shape beneath your breast,
Send from the heavens gleaming there,
To my disturbed spirit, rest.

Skylark who sing so clear, and light
Who stream upon me as I wake,
Shut from my memory thought of night,
And from my heart its sorrow take.

Sun who are burning far above,
Shine on my hapless soul a ray
Brighter than all the pain of love,
That I may smile and sing today!

VIVETTE HENDRIKS

The crow

Crows on the wing!
What grace as they swing,
Rising and diving
Like fish in the billows,
In the willowy air;
Or, softly as feathers
From broken pillows.

Crows on the wing;
What a symphony sings
The wind in their wings
As they swoop and they rise
To the sea: to the skies:
As they float in the light
Air, like fragments of night.

Crows on the wing:
See, their talons are red
With the blood from the head
Of a cow that they killed
In the old abattoir;
Like black thoughts of war,
Red-taloned: red-billed.

Crows on the wing:
As they watch and they wait,
Hovering . . . hovering,
Or sitting in state
On the abattoir roof,
For some beast's head or hoof,
Or watching their chances
From coco-nut branches.

Crows on the wing:
They remind me of men
Whose speech is as light
As the crow in their flight;
But whose fingers are red
With the blood of their brother!
The crows prey on the dead
But they prey on each other!

BARNABAS J. RAMON-FORTUNÉ

Sea bird

Scrawling a signature across
The map of the sky you fly
With the grace
Of warm memory
Touched with the scalpel of time past.

In the mosaic of the clouds
At sunset you fold proud
Wings to lie
Upon the palpitation of the waves

Leaving behind a tender trace
Of your lightness on the sand
For the careless sea to trod
On and erase.

Or in powered dives
With taut limpness down
The shafts of air your limbs
Sink in a sharp plunge
To the rocky ground.

Or rising from the catacombs
In an equipoise of wonderful
Propulsion your arms
Climb the tiers of the air
With an upward roll.

Your nest left huddled
In the ear of a rock
Mid the blast and wrack
Of fretful billows
Clamouring to be heard
You ride into the silence of the sky.

And far below you
As you soar
I envy your freedom
From the tug of time
Your glory
In the welfare of the air.

A. N. FORDE

Lines—written on a train

If, in response to the sobbing
Of wheels consuming miles of rail
Or the spirituals the peasants sing,
My heart were to flutter and reel

And my eyes to fill with tears,
He would not understand who sits
At my side and silently shares
The display of commonplace sights:

The fields where restless fires
Cause a horse to break his rope
And flee, erratic, through the choirs
That moving sing and singing reap

The canes; for mine and mine alone
Is the thought, that through the peasants' hearts—
Though they seem as callous as stone—
Some river runs which soothes their hurts,

While willy-nilly hearts like mine
Must roam ten thousand years of days
Afraid, lest with intractable whine
The river absorb the fire that slowly dies.

CECIL HERBERT

Holy

Holy be the white head of a Negro,
Sacred be the black flax of a black child.
Holy be
The golden down
That will stream in the waves of the winds
And will thin like dispersing cloud,
Holy be
Heads of Chinese hair
Sea calm sea impersonal
Deep flowering of the mellow and traditional.
Heads of peoples fair
Bright shimmering from the riches of their species;
Heads of Indians
With feeling of distance and space and dusk:
Heads of wheaten gold,
Heads of peoples dark
So strong so original:
All of the earth and the sun!

GEORGE CAMPBELL

Hidden ways

I have walked ways by velvet grass,
Walked in green places cityless,
Seen roses bloom
From grizzled twigs.

There in the quiet of the wild,
Lulled in beneficence of light,
Bough cracked limbs
Spread rich with fruit.

And on June mornings after rain,
Seen frail-stemmed vines in hidden tracks
Show strength in
Eloquence of flower.

These I have seen, and know indeed,
How the poor child of muffled chance
Can by adventure
Walk great ways.

HAROLD M. TELEMAQUE

Yes, I recall

Yes, I recall the sudden forsythia
Of early Spring
And white tunes, overwrought,
When snowflakes used to sing.

And in my dreams, the pines
I used to know
Still daub with shadows
The moon-blue snow.

JOHN FIGUEROA

Ave Maria

From a church across the street
    Children repeat
Hail Mary, full of Grace;
Skipping the syllables, Follow-the-Leader pace.

A little girl (the Lord is with Thee),
    White in organdy,
Lifts her starched, black face
    Towards the barricaded altar
Meadowed in lace.

(Blessed art Thou among women.)
    Her child's fingers string the coloured beads
One after one.
(Blessed is the fruit of Thy womb);
Yea, and blessed, too, ripe fruit on trees window-
    close,
    Under a tropical sun.

Bend low the laden bough
    Child-high; sweeten her incense-flavoured breath
With food, good Mary. (Holy Mary, Mother of God,
Pray for us sinners.) And for the blameless—
    Now, before the hour of their death.

BARBARA FERLAND

Spring feast

When the Roman soldier laughed
And showed his money
I was Magdalene.

When Judas counted coins
With double-entry envy,
Finding no means to appropriate,
I was he.

I was Peter
When he warmed himself
By the burning coals
And looked not at the accusing maid.

I was the darkened sun,
My heart the riven earth.
Now I am the Easter sun arisen.
The wind-tipped eagle
Scalloping across the sky.

Magdalene I was,
Judas, Peter;
Now I am the risen Lord.

JOHN FIGUEROA

All men come to the hills

All men come to the hills
Finally . . . .
Men from the deeps of the plains of the sea—
Where a wind-in-the sail is hope,
That long desire, and long weariness fulfills—
Come again to the hills.

And men with dusty, broken feet;
Proud men, lone men like me,
Seeking again the soul's deeps—
Or a shallow grave
Far from the tumult of the wave—
Where a bird's note motions the silence in. . . .
The white kiss of silence that the spirit stills
Still as a cloud of windless sail horizon-hung
    above the blue glass of the sea—
Come again to the hills. . . .
Come ever, finally.

ROGER MAIS

Sheep

God made sheep in the early morning.

In his hands he caught the clusters
Of the fleecy clouds of dawning
And tied them in bunches
And fastened their feet and their noses
With wet brown clay.

And into their eyes he dropped
With reeds from a nearby river
The light of the dying morning star
And the light of the dying moon.

And then on that creation morning
When the sun had flooded the peaks and plains
And the dew lay thick on the rushes
Man saw sheep on the grazing grass
And heard the sadness of their bleating.

K. E. INGRAM

Truth

Lord, shall I find it in Thy Holy Church,
Or must I give it up as something dead,
Forever lost, no matter where I search,
Like dinosaurs within their ancient bed?
I found it not in years of Unbelief,
In science stirring life like budding trees,
In Revolution like a dazzling thief—
Oh, shall I find it on my bended knees?

But what is Truth? So Pilate asked Thee, Lord,
So long ago when Thou wert manifest,
As the Eternal and Incarnate Word,
Chosen of God and by him singly blest:
In this vast world of lies and hate and greed,
Upon my knees, Oh Lord, for Truth I plead.

CLAUDE McKAY

The pagan isms

Around me roar and crash the pagan isms
To which most of my life was consecrate,
Betrayed by evil men and torn by schisms
For they were built on nothing more than hate!
I cannot live my life without the faith
Where new sensations like a faun will leap,
But old enthusiasms like a wraith,
Haunt me awake and haunt me when I sleep.

And so to God I go to make my peace,
Where black nor white can follow to betray.
My pent-up heart to Him I will release
And surely He will show the perfect way
Of life. For He will lead me and no man
Can violate or circumvent His plan.

CLAUDE MCKAY

Lullaby

Darkness broods on earth and air
Spilling shadows everywhere
Love lies dreaming Love is near
Lay your head to sleep

The crooked shadows bound and leap
Headlong through the looking-glass
Into nothingness they pass
Lay your head to sleep

Light will break in other guise
Colour blossom beneath skies
Where lamb with tawny lion lies
Lay your head to sleep

To-morrow Now and Yesterday
Slowly through the night will creep
All their harvest yours to reap
Lay your head to sleep

All the nightlong loveliness
Yours my darling to possess
And your soft-closed eyelids bless
Lay your head to sleep

FRANK COLLYMORE

Looking at your hands

No!
I will not still my voice!
I have
too much to claim—
if you see me
looking at books
or coming to your house
or walking in the sun
know that I look for fire!

I have learnt
from books dear friend
of men dreaming and living
and hungering in a room without a light
who could not die since death was far too poor
who did not sleep to dream, but dreamed to change
  the world

and so
if you see me
looking at your hands
listening when you speak
marching in your ranks
you must know
I do not sleep to dream, but dream to change the
  world.

MARTIN CARTER

A city's death by fire

After that hot gospeller had levelled all but the
    churched sky,
I wrote the tale by tallow of a city's death by fire;
Under a candle's eye, that smoked in tears, I
Wanted to tell, in more than wax, of faiths that
    were snapped like wire.
All day I walked abroad among the rubbled tales,
Shocked at each wall that stood on the street like a
    liar;
Loud was the bird-rocked sky, and all the clouds
    were bales
Torn open by looting, and white, in spite of the fire.
By the smoking sea, where Christ walked, I asked
    why
Should a man wax tears, when his wooden world
    fails?
In town, leaves were paper, but the hills were a flock
    of faiths;
To a boy who walked all day, each leaf was a green
    breath
Rebuilding a love I thought was dead as nails,
Blessing the death and the baptism by fire.

DEREK WALCOTT

At Easter

No winter in this equinoctial land, though the
    shrunken
Trees still share old rhythms;
Their emerald pales, through filigree of bated
Branches Orion marches westward,
And the grass is stubbly as an old toothbrush, thirsty
For rain. Then Easter comes and new
Life bursts from the dark tomb;
Gold is showered upon the blistered fence,
Gold gleams in the gutter; soon
Flamboyant's[1] arching flame will run
Along the backyard and the rusty lawn,
And the lilyblade be thrust from the grey mould.
Only a shower or two in the long interim
When day after day the windbare skies
Mock the tawny mantle of our land,
And foraging roots scrabble in dust.
Only a shower or two, and yet the miracle
Re-enacted; life unprisoned, beauty
Foiling dark bonds. The winds
Will soon despoil the gold, brief
Fruit for dreams; golden shower
And little crocuses all gone, gone
Back to oblivion. Always the cycle
Returning to rejoice parched hearts, each
Resurrection a remembrance, a valediction.

FRANK COLLYMORE

[1] Flamboyant: This poem comes from Barbados; in some other parts of the Caribbean the flamboyant plant is called the poincianna. (See footnote to "A mountain carved of bronze", page 57.)

Suggestions for Further Reading

Readers will find the poems which are mentioned here interesting and worthwhile. They are all connected in some way with the sections or separate poems in this book.

A list of the books referred to is given on pages 109–10. In some places public libraries will have these books, in other places schools will own some of them. English Departments in larger schools might well procure copies for reference. Some of them are published in quite inexpensive editions.

PART 1 PEOPLE

'Blue Girls' by John Crowe Ransom should be of interest (printed in *A Comprehensive Anthology of American Poetry*). See also Ezra Pound's translation from Rihaku which is called 'The River Merchant's Wife: A Letter'; and 'To Helen' by Edgar Allan Poe, which should be read along with 'Revelation' by H. A. Vaughan. 'Tarantella' by Hilaire Belloc should be read with 'Negro lass', as should be Vachel Lindsay's 'Congo'.

Another poem which should be of interest is Thomas Hardy's 'To Lizbie Browne' (printed in *Selected Poems of Thomas Hardy*). Hopkins' 'Felix Randall' is also well-worth looking at. It has connections with poems in this section and also, perhaps, with George Campbell's 'History makers' (page 66 of this anthology).

PART 2 NATURE

There is a great variety of poems that could be mentioned. Those from England which are likely to be best known are those by Wordsworth. But there are many poems by Robert Frost which would be well worth reading. And there is the poem 'Clover' by John Bannister Tabb, which has very much the feeling of 'Blue agave' by Frank Collymore. There is also 'Weathers' by Hardy (*Selected Poems of Thomas Hardy*); likewise 'To a Waterfowl' by William Cullen Bryant in *A Comprehensive Anthology of American Poetry*. Compare with George Campbell's 'Litany', Emily Dickinson's 'There's a certain slant of light' printed in *Selected Letters and Poems of Emily Dickinson*.

Another poem that may be looked at (along, for instance, with Claude McKay's 'Spring in New Hampshire') is Hopkins' 'Spring' printed in *Poems of Gerard Manley Hopkins*, edited by W. H. Gardner.

In temperate countries nature poetry is often concerned with the various seasons of the year. Many such poems will be well-known. But the reader might not have heard of the poem 'Seasons' which is to be found in *The Visitor of Mist*, a collection of poems by Jorge C. Andrade translated by G. R. Coulthard. 'An August Midnight' by Thomas Hardy in his *Selected Poems* contrasts well with 'June bug' by Edward Lucie-Smith. 'Confidence' by Marsden Hartley, printed in *A Comprehensive Anthology of American Poetry*, makes interesting reading in connection with J. R. Bunting's poem 'The pelican'.

PART 5   INTERLUDE

We often take poetry too seriously. It is, of course, worthy of respect because it is one of the great art forms, and has spoken to men and women throughout the ages. However, there is such a thing as good light verse. This anthology contains examples from the work of Frank Collymore. He himself has written other light verse; most of it can be found in *Bim*. The reader should find the following examples of light verse interesting: Hilaire Belloc's

'Cautionary Tales' and various of his epigrams—for instance his famous one which goes:

> 'He prayeth best who loveth best
> All things great and small.
> The diptycocus is the test—
> I love it least of all.'

Well-known is Lewis Carroll's 'Will you walk a little faster?' (*The Poet's Tongue*, Part 1). There is also a much less well-known poem on page 39 of part 1, and an amusing epigram which starts 'The common cormorant or shag . . . ' (no. 90). Edward Lear was of course a master of light verse; examples of his work appear in many anthologies, and readers old and young will enjoy his *Complete Nonsense* edited by Holbrook Jackson, and of course illustrated by Lear himself. T. S. Eliot's *Possum* poems should not be missed.

PART 6   BEYOND

There are, of course, many poems that could be referred to here. There is the very well-known poem by Robert Browning, 'Oh, to be in England now that April's here', in which Browning is looking back to his home with the same sort of feeling with which many West Indian poets think of their home when they are far away. For instance, Claude McKay's 'Spring in New Hampshire', and many of his other poems express this longing to return home. Note in this section 'At home the green remains' and 'The lament of the banana man'. Be sure to read Stephen Foster's 'My Old Kentucky Home' which is probably better known as a song, and which can be found in *A Comprehensive Anthology of American Poetry* edited by Conrad Aiken. Other well-known poems of this kind are: 'South Country' by Hilaire Belloc, and the medieval Latin poem 'Insula Felix', written from Fulda by Walafrid Strabo to his old master at Reichenau, and published in both Latin and English in Helen Waddell's *Medieval Latin Lyrics.*

There are many poems that are 'Beyond' in the sense that they deal with unusual experiences quite often of a religious kind. See, for instance, those by Emily Dickinson including 'Arcturus is his other name' in her *Selected Poems and Letters;* also Wordsworth's 'Lucy' poems; Robert Southwell's 'The Burning Babe' (*The Oxford Book of Sixteenth Century Verse*), and many of William Blake's poems, e.g. 'Mock on, Mock on, Voltaire, Rousseau', and 'And did those feet in ancient time'.

Frank Collymore's 'Lullaby' finds many echoes abroad. There is the well-known 'Cradle Song' by W. B. Yeats, 'Crying my little one' by Christina Rossetti in James Britton's *An Anthology of Verse for Children* (Book 1), 'Sweet and Low' by Tennyson, and 'A Cradle Song' by William Blake.

This book contains a few poems from the French-speaking Caribbean. The intention is simply to remind the reader that our French-speaking neighbours have concerns similar to ours, and have been writing poetry for a long time. No suggestion is intended that the poems here included are typical of poetry being written in the non-English-speaking Caribbean.

Most of these translations have been made by C. F. MacIntyre, who has also done well-received translations of Goethe, Rilke, Baudelaire, and others. The young reader might find of particular interest 'Piano Practice' and 'Dorcas Gazelle' which appear in his paperback translation of Rilke.

'The Conquistadores', translated by Vivian Virtue, is one of 118 connected sonnets by José-Maria de Heredia published together as *Les Trophées.* Mr Virtue is now translating the bulk of this work into English.

Further details about the books referred to above are given here. Some other useful anthologies have also been

mentioned, including collections by individual West
Indian poets.

AITKEN, Conrad, (ed.), *A Comprehensive Anthology of
American Poetry*, Random House (The Modern Library)
New York
ANDRADE, Jorge C., *The Visitor of Mist*, translated by
G. R. Coulthard, Williams & Norgate, London
AUDEN, W. H. and Garrett, John, *The Poet's Tongue*,
G. Bell & Sons, London, 1935
BELLOC, H., *Sonnets and Verse*, Duckworth, London
BRITTON, James, *An Anthology of Verse for Children*
(Books 1-4), Oxford University Press, London, 1957
ELIOT, T. S., *Selected Poems*, Penguin Books, Harmonds-
worth, 1948
ERSKINE, A. and Warren, R. P. (ed.), *Six Centuries of
Great Poetry*, Dell Publishing Co., New York, 1955
GARDNER, W. H. (ed.), *Poems of Gerald Manley Hopkins*,
Oxford University Press, London, 1948
GARRETT, J. and Auden, W. H., *The Poet's Tongue*, G. Bell
& Sons, London, 1935
GREENBERG, R. A. and Hepburn, J. C. (ed.), *Robert Frost:
An Introduction*, Holt, Rinehart & Winston, New York,
1961
HEPBURN, James C. and Greenberg, R. A. (ed.), *Robert
Frost: An Introduction*, Holt, Rinehart & Winston, New
York, 1961
JACKSON, Holbrook (ed.), *The Complete Nonsense of
Edward Lear*, Faber, London, 1947
LINSCOTT, Robert N. (ed.), *Selected Poems and Letters of
Emily Dickinson*, Doubleday & Company Inc., Garden
City, New York, 1959
MACBAIN, J. Murray (ed.), *The Book of a Thousand Poems*,
Evans Brothers, London
MACINTYRE, C. F. (ed.), *Rilke*, University of California
Press, Berkeley and Los Angeles
RANSOM, John Crowe (ed.), *Selected Poems of Thomas
Hardy*, The Macmillan Co., New York, 1961

WADDELL, Helen (ed.), *Medieval Latin Lyrics*, Penguin Books, Harmondsworth, 1952

WARREN, Robert Penn and Erskine, A. (ed.), *Six Centuries of Great Poetry*, Dell Publishing Co., New York, 1955

See also:

BRATHWAITE, Edward, *The Arrivants*, Oxford University Press, London, 1973; *Other Exiles*, Oxford University Press, London 1975

BROWN, Wayne, *On The Coast*, André Deutsch, London 1972

CAMPBELL, George, *First Poems*, City Printery Ltd., Kingston, Jamaica, 1945

CARTER, Martin, *Poems of Succession*, New Beacon Books, London, 1977

FIGUEROA, John, *Ignoring Hurts*, Three Continents Press Inc., Washington, D.C.

LUCIE-SMITH, Edward, *Tropical Childhood*, Oxford University Press, London, 1961

McKAY, Claude, *Harlem Shadows* (introduction by Max Eastman), Harcourt Brace & Co., New York, 1922

McNEIL, A., Reel from 'The Life Movie', *Savacou*, January 1975

MORDECAI, Pamela and Morris, Mervyn (ed.), *Jamaica Woman*, Heinemann Educational Books (Caribbean), 1980

MORRIS, Mervyn, *Shadow Boxing*, New Beacon Books, London

SCOTT, Dennis, *Uncle Time*, University of Pittsburgh Press, 1973

WALCOTT, Derek, *In a Green Light*, Jonathan Cape, London, 1962; *Another Life*, Jonathan Cape, London, 1973; *Star-Apple Kingdom*, Farrar, Straus & Giroux Inc., New York, 1977

and

'A Caribbean Sampler', *Bim*, Vol. 5, No. 20, June 1954, St. Michael, Barbados

'A West Indian Anthology', *Kyk-over-al*, Vol. IV, No. 14, Georgetown, Guyana

Index of Authors and Titles

WILLIAM ARTHUR is a schoolmaster and lives in Barbados. Born 1909 Barbados.
Negro lass *12*

J. R. BUNTING, at one time Headmaster of Wolmer's Boys' School, Jamaica; an Englishman who lived for many years in Jamaica and Nigeria. Born 1929 England.
The pelican *36*

GEORGE CAMPBELL, a gifted Jamaican poet who has recently returned, after many years in New York, to live in Jamaica. He first came to notice at the time of the 1937-8 'troubles' in Jamaica. After many years of silence he has just published a new collection of poems. Born 1918 Jamaica.
Constitution Day poem *67*
Drought *33*
History makers *66*
Holy *94*
Litany *27*

H. D. CARBERRY, a Jamaican lawyer and collector of Caribbean books. Studied at Oxford and the Inns of Court. President of West Indian Students' Union, London in the 1950s. Born 1921 Montreal, Canada of Jamaican parentage.
A mountain carved of bronze *56*
Nature *25*
My country grows *64*

JAN CAREW, an established novelist and academic from Guyana; has travelled widely in Africa and Europe. Has now settled in the U.S.A. where he has done much to promote Caribbean and African studies. Born 1925 Guyana.
Alone *85*
Chaotic epic *16*

MARTIN CARTER is from Guyana where he lives and where, from time to time, he has served in the Government. Born 1827 Guyana.
Looking at your hands *102*

FRANK COLLYMORE, Grand Old Man of West Indian letters, editor of *Bim*, Barbados. His work was described and honoured in *Savacou* 8/9. Honoured by U.W.I. and the Queen. Born 1893 Barbados, died 1980.

FRANK COLLYMORE—*continued*
At Easter   104
Blue agave   24
Flying fish   81
Lullaby   101
Poem   50
The butterfly   81
The coral polyp   80
The mongoose   81
The moth   81
The spider   80
Triptych   62
Turkeys   80

NEVILLE DAWES, Jamaican novelist; worked in Ghana for many years. Recently Secretary of the Jamaica Institute. Born 1926 Warri, Nigeria of Jamaican parentage.
Fugue   23

GILBERT DE CHAMBERTRAND is from Gaudeloupe. During a varied career he has been journalist, artist, novelist, poet and playwright. Born 1890 Guadeloupe, died 1973.
Terre-de-Hauts-des-Saintes   31

JOSÉ-MARIA DE HEREDIA was born in Cuba and settled in France where he became one of the leaders of the Parnassian movement and a member of the Academie Française. Born 1803 Cuba, died 1839.
The Conquistadores   70

GEOFFREY DRAYTON lives and works in Barbados. Born 1924 Barbados.
Seeds of the pomegranate   60

GLORIA ESCOFFERY, a Jamaican who has lived in England, Canada and Barbados. She is now settled at home and is one of Jamaica's outstanding painters. Born 1923 Jamaica.
Spring   27
The shoemaker   12

BARBARA FERLAND is a Jamaican, now living in England. Born 1919 Jamaica.
Ave Maria   96
Hibiscus   36

JOHN FIGUEROA, Jamaican poet and academic. For seventeen years Professor of Education, U.W.I. Travelled extensively in

Africa and the Americas. Now in Third World Studies, The Open University, England. Born 1920.
At home the green remains . . . 84
On hearing Dvorak's 'New World' Symphony 52
Spring feast 97
Yes, I recall 95

A. N. FORDE is a poet and Civil Servant from Barbados. An editor of *Bim*, who has taught in Tobago and Grenada. Born 1923 Barbados.
Sea Bird 91

GILBERT GRATIANT is from Martinique, a lecturer in English now living in France. Born 1895 Martinique.
To Schoelcher 3

G. A. HAMILTON is from Jamaica.
Thoughts of Port Royal 71

VIVETTE HENDRIKS, a Jamaican now living in Ireland. Born 1925 Jamaica.
Prayer at morning 89

CECIL HERBERT, a gifted poet from Trinidad who has not published extensively. Born 1926 Trinidad.
And the pouis sing 72
Lines—written on a train 93

ERROL HILL, a Trinidadian, expert on West Indian Theatre, has worked in Jamaica and Africa. Now Professor at Dartmouth College, U.S.A. Born 1921 Trinidad.
Beggarman 8

CONSTANCE HOLLAR was one of Jamaica's first women poets. Sister to the well-known Jamaican classical scholar and teacher, Anna Hollar. Born 1880 Jamaica, died 1945.
A leaf from the tree of darkness 28
Gold are the fruit of night 39

K. E. INGRAM, a Jamaican just retiring as Librarian at the University of the West Indies, Mona. Born 1921 Jamaica.
It is a rose-red morning 2
Sheep 98

EVAN JONES, a Jamaican who has lived and taught in the U.S.A. Has settled in England where he writes scripts for T.V. and films. Born 1927 Jamaica.
The lament of the banana man 86
The song of the banana man 4

KNOLLY S. LA FORTUNÉ is from Trinidad. Born 1920 Trinidad.
Theresa, return to me   *18*

GEORGE LAMMING, one of the Caribbean's outstanding novelists. Left Barbados as a youth to work in Trinidad. Subsequently lived and worked in England. Has lectured at universities in Africa and the U.S.A. Now back in Barbados. Born 1927 Barbados.
Song for Marion   *19*

ARCHIE LINDO is from Jamaica. Born 1919 Jamaica.
Time for digging   *38*

MARY LOCKETT is from Jamaica. Born 1872 Jamaica.
Weather in action   *34*

EDWARD LUCIE-SMITH was born in Jamaica where he spent his early years. Has made his home in England where he is a well-known and respected poet and critic. Born 1933 Jamaica.
June bug   *65*

BASIL McFARLANE is a Jamaican whose father, the late J. Clare McFarlane, was formerly poet laureate of the island. Born 1922 Jamaica.
Music a kind of sleep   *88*
The modern man   *11*

C. F. MACINTYRE, a well-known American poet and translator who lived for many years in Paris.
Consecration of the serpents (*translation*)   *68*
Terre-de-Hauts-des-Saintes (translation)   *31*
To Schoelcher (translation)   *3*
To the Antilles (translation)   *82*

CLAUDE McKAY left Jamaica as a young man and spent the rest of his life in the U.S.A. (except for long visits to Russia and France) where he became famous as a poet and novelist. Born 1889 Jamaica, died 1948.
Jasmine   *83*
Like a strong tree   *88*
My mother   *14*
On Broadway   *83*
Poetry   *49*
Spring in New Hampshire   *87*
The pagan isms   *100*
The tropics in New York   *82*
Truth   *99*

ROGER MAIS lived most of his life in Jamaica, but spent a few years in Europe and England. Also a novelist and painter. Born

1905 Jamaica, died 1955.
All men come to the hills *98*
Children coming from school *2*
Night comes *26*

UNA MARSON, a Jamaican who was prominent in BBC
broadcasting to the West Indies during the war; prime mover in
the League of Coloured People, England. Born 1905 Jamaica,
died 1965.
Darlingford *32*

STELLA MEAD, an English authoress and journalist who has
lived and worked in Jamaica, France, Germany and India.
St. Andrew Hills *37*

REGINALD M. MURRAY, a famous Jamaican headmaster who
retired in the early 1940's. Born 1900, died 1964.
The Palisadoes Peninsula *68*

DAISY MYRIE is a Jamaican. Born 1908 Jamaica.
Marketwomen *10*

ALFRED PRAGNELL is a well-known broadcaster in Barbados.
Born 1925.
In memoriam *17*

BARNABAS J. RAMON-FORTUNÉ is from Trinidad. Born
1905 Trinidad.
The crow *90*
The riders *1*
The word once spoken *55*

CARL RATTRAY is from Jamaica.
Mid-year *34*

E. M. ROACH, outstanding poet and journalist. Born 1918
Tobago, died 1974.
February *21*

A. J. SEYMOUR is one of the 'god-fathers' of Caribbean Litera-
ture. Worked for a few years in Puerto Rico with the Central
Secretariat of the Caribbean Organization. He has lived most of
his life in Guyana where he has been a staunch member of the
Methodist Church and a gentle promoter of the arts. Editor of
Kyk-over-al. Born 1914 Guyana.
For Christopher Columbus *74*
Over Guiana, clouds *40*

P. M. SHERLOCK is a Jamaican writer and educationist who
was formerly Vice-Chancellor of the University of the West

116

Index of First Lines